FRISCO!

FRISCO

HISTORICAL

SOCIETY

A Colorful Colorado Community

By Mary Ellen Gilliland

Library of Congress Catalog Card Number: 84-71449

ISBN: 0-9603624-3-6

This book is a publishing project of the Frisco Historical Society.

 FRISCO   HISTORICAL   SOCIETY
Box 820
Frisco, Colorado 80443
(303) 668-5276

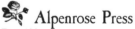 Alpenrose Press
Box 499
Silverthorne, Colorado 80498
(303) 468-6273

CONTENTS

Acknowledgments

The author wishes to thank the Frisco Historical Society for providing research materials, for painstaking editorial effort and for its commitment to the excellence of this book. Those who generously contributed time, memories or manuscipt critique were Jody Anderson, Wayne and Lola Mae Bristol, Kenneth Caldwell, Sue Chamberlain, Harold Deming, Reverend Mark and Roberta Fiester, Helen Foote, Howard and Lura Belle Giberson, Doug Jones, Patricia Foote Masters, Henry and Sharon Recen, Paul and Beverly Recen, Captain and Susan Thompson, William Wildhack and Marie Zdechlik. C. Philip Johnson gave his kind permission to use Belle Turnbull's poems. The author used information from Ann and Don English's detailed Frisco research paper, "The Successful Miner" along with personal research files. Thanks are extended to Janet Marie Clawson for help with photo research. Mary Katherine Trevithick, Papillon Graphics, and Billie Geist, The Art Workers, gave generous help. I express my warmest thanks for the many others who shared remembrances of early Frisco during casual conversations, telephone calls and through their wonderful letters. Special appreciation goes to Larry Gilliland for manuscript preparation/typesetting on a microcomputer.

M. E. G.

CHAPTER 1

A Town Is Born

The Great Divide is a full-sprung bow
About that country, and its arrow
Is the length of the Tenmile, notch to tip.
Stark is the Streamhead where the narrow
Careless snowrills stop and go,
Atlantic, Pacific, freeze or flow.
(Belle Turnbull, *The Tenmile Range*)

Frisco's fascinating story began with staunch nineteenth century capitalists who founded the town—and found silver on their rocky doorstep. Saloons and stores prospered and two gutsy narrow-gauge mountain railways competed to serve Frisco. Around 1900, a Civil War colonel struck gold here. Frisco floated on high times until 1910, when the mining bubble burst. Then the never-say-die community became a happy "hometown America" place where people loved to live. Isolated Frisco remained for years locked in nineteenth century ways. Suddenly, post-war changes, including the ski industry's momentous birth, catapulted a Rip Van Winkle community into the vibrant twentieth century. Follow Frisco's colorful march through time. The story begins in tranquility, untroubled as the womb.

The Land Lay Waiting

The spacious, two-mile-square mountain park that became Frisco's site in later mining boom days lay sleeping during the firecracker explosion of Colorado's gold rush. After Ruben J. Spalding pushed over the range to make the Western slope's first placer gold strike on the Blue River August 10, 1859, the Valley of the Blue swarmed with pick 'n pan prospectors washing, digging and sluicing placer gold nuggets, flakes, flecks and dust. Yet Frisco's mountain-rimmed basin, flat and open as a gold pan at 9,097 feet altitude, waited undisturbed. While hordes of frenzied gold seekers scrambled over the craggy Continental Divide to boost a newborn Breckenridge's population to 8,000 by spring, 1860, the serene meadow at

1

the Ten Mile Canyon's mouth continued to doze.

...No hasty tent saloons thrown up for thirsty newcomers by men with eyes glittering gold... No shanty log dancehalls and rough-hewn five-to-a-bed boarding houses in helter-skelter confusion... No motley crew of claimjumpers, shyster lawyers, loafers, gamblers and madams invaded the tranquil valley. The land lay in virgin repose.

Geologic Treasure Trove: Gold and Glaciers

Sentinel peaks surrounding the site, 12,805-foot Peak One, 10,502-foot Mount Royal, 10,855-foot Wichita and 10,880-foot Chief Mountain, had guarded the valley for eons. The rocky-spired Ten Mile range stretches from Frisco's Peak One to Breckenridge, where Peak Ten pushes to almost 14,000 feet. The Gore range guards Frisco's west boundary. Both ranges are ancient. Their Precambrian granite and gneiss formed 600 million years ago. A mere 70 million years back, a violent geologic upheaval jarred the ancient rock into a mosaic of fractures. As the floor of the earth opened, a fiery cauldron of lava, hot water and gases spewed forth. Into the cracked, fissured and split Precambrian rock pushed boiling streams from the earth's rich storehouse—fingers of gold, silver, lead, zinc and copper. The valley that would host the town ages later stood surrounded by mountains striped with hidden veins of precious metal. Frisco would straddle a 240-mile long Colorado mineral belt that later spawned Gold Hill, Idaho Springs, Central City, Black Hawk, Empire, Montezuma, Breckenridge and Leadville, mineral camps that created legends.

A 1,000-foot wide river of ice pushed an easy path through the Blue River Valley during the Ice Age. Soft sedimentary rock laid down by prehistoric muds of an ancient Inland Sea gave the advancing glacier an easy ride. Not so in Frisco's steep-walled Ten Mile Canyon. There a massive ice flow labored through a huge single mountain range to carve a deep canyon. Geologists assert that the Ten Mile and Gore ranges joined as one before the canyon formed. Halka Chronic's *Roadside Geology of Colorado* states, "In terms of geologic structure, these two ranges are continuous, faults... can be traced right across the Ten Mile Canyon." Gold and silver veins run across the canyon as well.

Colorado's Real "Natives"

For the Ute Indians, a Colorado mountain tribe, the canyon glacier and its successor, the tumbling, boulder-strewn Ten Mile River,

2

created a handy route between hunting grounds. The short, stocky, dark-skinned Ute hunted elk, deer and bison atop nearby Vail Pass, archeologists say, then headed down the Ten Mile Canyon to a favorite camp on the site of today's Frisco. Often the nomad Utes continued south along the Blue to buffalo pastures and winter habitation sites in South Park, over the range from Breckenridge.

These Indians, and their ancestors before them, traveled the Frisco route for almost 7,000 years. Construction crews building the I-70 highway over Vail Pass unearthed a prehistoric Indian camp near the pass' 10,601-foot summit that Smithsonian Institute scientists carbon-dated back 6,800 years. Archeologists unearthed bone fragments from wild game, arrowheads, ceramic pieces and fragments from wood scrapers, knives, hammerstones and choppers. The one-quarter mile camp site served Indians continuously from 4,800 BC to about 1,760 AD.

Ute Indians also traveled a trail along the Blue River that made the Frisco meadowlands a convenient camp. The route along the Blue linked their "spirit lake" in Grand County to the north with South Park. "Indians were seen frequently in the summer going from Middle Park to South Park...but they did not molest the whites," a 1936 *Summit County Journal* article recalled.

Grandmother Recen
Recen Family Photo

3

Beaver Men

Finally, in the early 1800s, American fur trappers penetrated the isolated reaches of the valley the nomad Utes called Nah-oon-kara (translated roughly as "land where the Blue River rises"). The basin that later became Frisco and its nearby canyons, provided just what the buckskin-clad, pipe-smoking, knife-wielding trapper wanted. Icy high-country beaver ponds made the musky-scented mammal grow fur thick enough to match the altitude and climate—the perfect pelt for a fancy gentleman's beaver fur hat.

During the fur trade years, 1810-1840, the area provided a favored lair for the rugged trappers. Early cartographers showed a rendevous site "at the place where the rivers meet," called La Bonte's Hole, located beneath the present Dillon Reservoir.

First Tourists

Trappers' moccasined footprints probably formed the white man's first impact on this mountain region. But U. S. explorers also mapped the Rockies. Among them stands Colonel John C. Fremont, the famous "Pathfinder," who described Frisco's environs in the diary of his 1843 expedition:

> In the afternoon the river forked into three apparently equal streams. The Snake, Blue and Ten Mile rivers... I proceeded up the middle branch [the Blue River], which formed a flat valley bottom between timbered ridges on the left and snowy mountains on the right [the Ten Mile Range] terminating on large buttes of naked rock.

Later visitors, including 1860s newsman Samuel Bowles, remembered the site which became Frisco. "Ten Mile Creek overflows with trout," reported Bowles in his 1869 *Colorado: Its Parks and Mountains.* "General Lord took ten pounds out of a single hole in a less number of minutes,—a single fish weighing about three pounds."

Almost upon the heels of Samuel Bowles came another visitor, Swedish-born Henry A. Recen. This one, a stonemason turned prospector, arrived in the spring of 1871 and decided to stay. He cut aspens to construct a cabin on a beautiful island at the confluence of the Ten Mile and North Ten Mile Creek (today's Ten Mile Island). His son, Henry A. Recen, later wrote, "Then my father located his first mining claim, the Juno Lode, on the left just at the mouth of the Ten Mile Canyon."

The Juno became the first of a string of rich silver strikes that made Henry Recen, and his brothers Andrew and Daniel, famous

Henry A. Recen

1848-1914

A merica's streets were paved with silver for a young Swede named Henry Recen (Ray-seen) during Colorado's storied mineral boom days. Recen, who built Frisco's first cabin, came to the U. S. from Lysvik in north central Sweden, stopping first in Lawrence, Kansas' Swedish community, then in Central City, Colorado. A stonemason by trade, Recen laid bricks for Blackhawk's first smelter and stone for the famous Central City Opera House, an 1800s cultural hub still attracting celebrities today. When he struck it rich at Idaho Springs' Elephant Mine (his $5,000 yield meant a small fortune in the 1870s), and then explored the rich Ten Mile Canyon in 1871, an exuberant Henry Recen hurried back to Sweden to bring his brothers to Colorado's silver-latticed land of promise.

Recen married Catherine Matson during that 1876 visit to Sweden. Then, he, his bride and brothers Daniel and Andrew sailed for America. They left behind a fourth brother, Per, who would be denied immigration papers at Ellis Island because of a club foot. Catherine Matson, according to her son, Henry A. Recen, Jr., was "the first white woman through the Ten Mile Canyon." She rode horseback on an old Indian trail.

5

Daniel Recen promptly discovered the dazzling Queen of the West Mine, December 28, 1878, on Jacque Peak, one of the Ten Mile Canyon's richest lodes, producing over half a century's yield of rich silver ores. Andrew struck silver at the adjoining Enterprise Lode. Dan later sold his mine for a then-impressive $80,000 and discovered the Excelsior. The rich young Recen tarried with 1870s silver magnates, such as H. A. W. Tabor, and celebrities, such as singer Jenny Lind. He and Andrew hired private rail cars for bachelor parties, extravagant with champagne, oysters and socialite guests.

Meanwhile, the hard-working Henry located his Frisco mine, the Juno Lode, and worked with his brothers on the Herculean Bar Placer, just below the frenzied 1879 boom town of Kokomo. When Kokomo burned in 1881, the 1,500-strong community relocated at Recen, a town the brothers platted in 1878 on their placer claim.

Henry and Catherine Recen raised three children, Julia, 1882; Henry A. Recen, Jr., 1883; and Albert, 1886. Catherine died unexpectedly before Albert's first birthday and Henry Recen persuaded his Swedish mother to travel to Kokomo to raise the Recen brood.

Henry's bachelor brothers, meanwhile, kicked up their heels until the 1893 silver crash, coupled with bad investments, left them almost penniless. The brothers trapped and prospected in the rugged Gore Range wilderness, building a small cabin on Gore Creek. They each died alone there, Andrew in 1912 and Daniel in 1917. Henry Recen died in 1914. His son, H. A., Jr., went up to bury old Dan beside his brother's grave under the pines. (The marked graves still remain on the Gore Creek hiking trail.) An October blizzard blew in and Henry, Jr. waded through deep drifts on his return, arriving at Frisco's Excelsior Mine exhausted and able to get no farther. Eyvind Flood put him to bed and prepared a hot meal to revive the young Recen.

Henry Recen, Jr. became one of Summit County's best-known citizens. Kokomo's longtime mayor and a 1920s and '30s county commissioner, Recen excelled at a variety of vocations—as machinist, tool and die maker, miner, geologist and surveyor. Recen surveyed the present Loveland Pass route in 1920, according to the May 29, 1963 *Rocky Mountain News*. He perfected his machinist and tool-making skills at Breckenridge's famous Gold Pan (later Tonopah) Shops. A talented artist and creator, Recen also invented many devices, from his energy-conscious "perpetual motion machine" to an instrument designed to help prospectors identify ore veins. A precise man with impeccable manners, he always dressed in a natty coat and tie, and was always freshly shaved, even in his rough mine town locale. "When Uncle Henry danced with a lady," said his Denver nephew, Paul Recen, "he always placed a clean handkerchief over his hand, so he would not dampen his partner's back with any sign of perspiration." Like his uncles, Andrew and Daniel, he remained a bachelor. "He never overate," and "he never cussed" and "he put rubber bands on everthing—his wallet, his glasses case, his letters," added Paul Recen's wife, Beverly. Paul's brother and wife, Henry A. and Sharon Recen, remembered that even as an old man, Henry Recen, Jr. "walked down the street so fast that you couldn't keep up with him." Henry, like his father, was a deeply spiritual man. "He was buried with his Bible," his Frisco friends recalled.

Both father and son also shared faith in the Meridian Mine, a 1500 by 600-foot claim on Mt. Royal's rocky north face. The Recens never gave up their conviction that the claim hid gold in its craggy confines. When the father-son team came close to their big strike, the deep tunnel flooded with groundwater, barricading the gold so close at hand.

The Denver Recens, grandsons of pioneer, Henry, Sr. by his son, Albert, can swap stories about the family from dawn till the sun sets over the barren waste of what was once Kokomo-Recen. (Climax tore down the town to create a tailings pond.) They talk about when Recen's Ten Mile Island cabin, Frisco's first, burned. Only the barrel of Henry, Sr.'s Sharp's rifle remained in the ash. A valuable diamond ring, owned by a visiting friend from Sweden, never turned up in the ruins. They recalled stories about Great-grandmother Recen, who came to Colorado to raise the Recens speaking only Swedish. Arthritic, she hobbled along with two canes, despite her large, powerful build. When Henry, Jr. prepared to depart for school in Frisco as a young boy, he always took Grandmother's spool and threaded several needles before leaving, for the old Swedish lady had nearly gone blind.

Daniel Recen

Andrew Recen
Recen Family Photo

in the annals of Ten Mile Canyon mining. Dan Recen took a fortune out from his fabled Queen of the West and sold the mine, according to nephew Henry Recen, Jr. The Recen Lode, the Herculean Bar Placer, the St. Louis, Frisco's Excelsior Mine and the Meridian Lode on Frisco's Mount Royal number among the pioneering Recen brothers' chain of discoveries.

What's In A Name?

Plenty in the case of Frisco. The name echoes the frenzied pitch of California's gold rush, the bawdiness of a boom town, the high hopes of eager arrivals from around the nation and the globe. But Frisco's name also created a mystery, a puzzle that was solved only at the town's 100th birthday!

Henry Recen played a big part in the secret by not being at home the day a former government scout passed by in 1875. On impulse, the visitor tacked up a sign, with the carved name, "Frisco City," over Recen's door. Then the scout, whose name was remembered as "Captain Leonard" passed into obscurity. Or at least we thought so.

Colorado historians proceeded to have a heyday with the mysterious "Captain Leonard" and the story of Frisco's name. Perry Eberhart's *Guide to Colorado Ghost Towns and Mining Camps* insists Captain Leonard built the cabin himself and named Frisco. Local historians published a pamphlet attributing the name "Frisco

House" to practical joker Leonard, who named the cabin after an infamous Leadville red light parlor. Most historians simply report the cabin sign and describe Captain Leonard as an Indian Scout with an ability to disappear.

Like many mysteries, this one is quite simple. A misspelling in Leonard's name obscured the government agent's true identity as Captain Henry Learned, an 1879 Frisco town founder, former scout, civil war veteran and an early town mayor, postmaster, school board organizer and mine owner. The vanishing 1875 visitor became a staunch and solid Frisco citizen who would guide the town through both boom and bust until his death over a quarter century later.

Timing: Frisco's Success Secret

Colorado in 1878 stood on the brink of a boom unprecedented in the state's already dazzling history. When the explosion hit, the sleepy mountain park named "Frisco City" would burst into life.

Placer mining had played out in gold- and silver-seamed Colorado. The rush following 1858 on Denver's Cherry Creek and 1859 on the Western Slope had fizzled. Nobody thought much about hard-rock mining. Dynamite and compressed air mining drills hadn't been invented. But in 1878 miners in Leadville struck silver lodes that rocked Colorado with news of their richness. Summit '59er Will Iliff quickly followed with a gold vein at his Breckenridge-area Blue Danube Mine. Leadville prospectors swarmed over Fremont Pass to uncover vein after vein of stunning silver strikes in the upper Ten Mile Canyon. Population mushroomed. Carpenters' hammers banged into the night raising new towns like the Canyon's Kokomo and Robinson. And savvy businessmen gathered together to form a company to buy a townsite at Frisco.

Frisco had three big bonuses:

Transportation crossroads: Frisco stood at the junction of two vital 1860s-built wagon roads, the Argentine Pass route from Georgetown and the Breckenridge Pass route (later named Boreas) from Denver. More importantly, William Austin Hamilton Loveland, Colorado Central railroad magnate, planned to link his rail terminus at Georgetown with Summit County and silver-rich Leadville. The new Loveland Pass road eliminated 70 miles from existing Denver to Leadville routes. An impatient Loveland launched road construction in deep snow in February, 1879. When the 60-mile dirt track stood complete in June, 1879, Frisco lay smack at the mid-point of a newly planned stagecoach route.

FRISCO!

Here comes the Railroad!: Denver & Rio Grande Railway officials shared inside knowledge with Frisco's founders that a D&RG branch from Leadville would soon penetrate the Ten Mile Canyon via Fremont Pass to the prospective townsite.

Mines: H. A. Recen's pioneering Juno vein, the lower Ten Mile Canyon's first lode, led the way for successive strikes in the Frisco area. Frisco's appropriately-named Golden Gate Mining and Milling Company, along with the Frisco Discovery and Mining Company, emerged first on the fledgling town's mining scene. Enthusiastic prospectors scrambled over snow-blanketed peaks during the 1878-79 winter to make the initial discoveries, then proved their strikes the following summer, according to the *Summit County Leader*. Denver newspapers breathlessly reported on Frisco's earliest mines including the New York, Frisco Belle, Ten Mile Chief, Mogul, Mermaid and Victoria.

The *Denver Daily Tribune* heralded the new town, 1,500-acre "Frisco City," in an April 5, 1879 announcement:

> Mr. W. A. Rand, agent for Denver, Golden, Boulder and Leadville parties, has secured a large tract of land for this company. Captain Henry Learned, agent for some of the principal businessmen at Lawrence, Kansas selected the site.

Capitalists Lay Cornerstone

With a 150 acre federally-granted townsite and investment dollars to purchase 1,350 acres surrounding, a hotel, sawmill, saloon, store, corral and feed stable under construction, plus plans for an ore smelter, energetic Frisco founders had themselves a town. The group filed incorporation papers for their new investment company, The Frisco Town Association, on April 17, 1879, according to the April 18 *Rocky Mountain News*.

> The Frisco Town Association filed articles of incorporation with the Secretary of State yesterday morning. The company organizes for the purpose of surveying and laying out a town site on the Ten Mile Creek in Summit County. The capital stock of the company is to be $5000, divided into shares of $50 each.

An initial problem, which in no way dampened the spirits of Frisco's founders, was mail delivery. Those anxious for a letter could travel the 10 miles south to Breckenridge or 14 miles to the new town of Kokomo. The nearest postoffice west, according to Henry

Recen, was Salt Lake City. But the indefatigable Frisco founders wangled a postoffice in little time. On August 15, 1879, a new Frisco postoffice opened to serve 50 town residents and 100 in the canyons nearby. Boulder transplant and town investor Peter Leyner, who had the unusual distinction of being a Colorado native in a nearly new state, stepped into his post as Frisco's first postmaster on August 29. Leyner, whose flourishing penmanship embellishes the 1879 postal documents, would remain in Frisco as a town leader and hotel owner.

In March, 1880, the *Rocky Mountain News* tantalized readers with the hottest news in mining opportunities near Frisco. The *News* listed a number of new strikes and the excited New York and Chicago capitalists anxious to invest in them.

By July, a growing town earned this appraisal by the *Central City Daily Register:*

> Frisco is a new camp and stage station, consisting of eight or nine cabins, stables, sawmills, etc. Rich carbonates have been found at a depth of 17 feet nearby.

The *News* in September, 1880 praised the high moral fiber of Frisco's populace. The report classed "fallen women" with clerics: "Frisco at present is entirely free of lawyers, gamblers, fallen women and ministers."

Residents waited a year to begin the process of incorporating their new town. Forty-nine Frisco citizens voted unanimously on September 7, 1880 for town incorporation. The town's first general election, held in David C. Crowell's Frisco House hotel office on September 29, 1880, established B. B. Babcock, a 28-year old unmarried prospector, as mayor. Virginia-born D. C. Crowell, whose beautiful script graces the early town records, was elected recorder. Voters selected as first town trustees Ohio-born lumber yard owner C. F. Shedd; 50-year old English miner John Doble; John Garrison; and J. S. Scott, a railroad mechanic from Golden, Colorado.

The *Denver Tribune* on December 4, 1880 reported Frisco had filed incorporation papers with the Colorado Secretary of State on December 3. The newspaper reported that Frisco lay at the proposed terminus of the Rio Grande railroad, a big boost for any new community's business life.

Progress Makes a Mighty Racket

The bustling town had quickly sold 150 town lots. (Cost $5, or $10 for a corner site.) Town fathers reserved a lot for a future Summit

FRISCO!

County courthouse, a move brimming with the optimism of the day. A cacophony of sawing, hammering, squeaking freight wagon wheels and neighing workhorse teams assaulted the ears of residents as construction racket accompanied the rise of building after building. Most splendid was Peter Leyner's September, 1880-completed hotel, The Leyner House, large enough for 50 guests. (Leyner had humbler beginnings. He had housed his family in a tent in 1879 while erecting Frisco's first building, a large log stable.) Frisco boasted two additional hotels, the Frisco House and the Stafford. Three general stores, erected during the town's first year, competed for residents' needs in grocery and mining supplies. Charles F. Shedd launched his second business, a general store. His bonanza lumber yard already turned out a lucrative 10,000 feet of lumber per day in 1880. J. S. Scott opened a "first class" general merchandise store as did Doble & Stokes. Adolphus "Tip" Baliff, an 1879 stagecoach driver on Nott's "High Line," settled in Frisco to build a blacksmith shop.

Like its Golden Gate namesake, Frisco attracted newcomers from eleven states and European nations, such as England, Ireland, Switzerland and Scotland.

Hurrah for the High Line!

Frisco basked in immediate success. Silas W. Nott's aggressive High Line stagecoach service played a key role in Frisco's immediate growth. Nott launched his tri-weekly passenger and express stagecoach service from Georgetown as far as Kokomo in June, 1879—a blessed coincidence for a fledgling Frisco, born at the same time. The stage whisked passengers from the railroad depot in Georgetown up and over the just-completed Loveland Pass road and on to Frisco each Monday, Wednesday and Friday, according to the June 26, 1879 *Georgetown Courier*. Stages returned from Kokomo on Tuesday, Thursday, and Saturday. Fare: $7.00.

In July, Mr. Nott snared a U. S. postal service contract to carry daily mails from Georgetown to Kokomo. Frisco received daily stage service and daily mail as soon as its postoffice opened in August. By September, 1879, Nott had purchased and put to harness three double six-horse teams and a trio of brand-new Concord coaches. The *Georgetown Courier* praised his drivers as "the best in the Rocky Mountains." Neither raging winter storms, nor Loveland Pass avalanches, nor fetlock-deep spring mud deterred Silas Nott. When business boomed enough to run 100 horses and three or four High Line stages daily, Frisco became a layover point on a route extended

*Sure-footed burros carried
miners, ore sacks and gear to and
from Summit's challenging mine
locations.*

to Leadville.

A stream of visitors poured out from the plush interiors of Concord coaches to hunt gold nuggets and enjoy the hospitality of Frisco's three hotels. Advertisements named Frisco as "Halfway Stop," because the town lay 32 miles from Georgetown and 32 miles from Leadville. Nott's branch line to Breckenridge, round-trip in one day, left Frisco at 9 a.m. daily.

No Lusty Mine Camp

Thus, a town was born, and one unique to Summit County's gold rush days growth. Breckenridge and Montezuma, Kokomo and Robinson (the last two are now gone), began in bawdy squalor, with saloons in hastily thrown-up tents and cabins built smack in the middle of what would be Main Street. The neer-do-wells that followed in the prospector's wake— gamblers, pettifoggers, dance-hall girls, shysters and quacks— created havoc over and above the choking dust, polluted waterways and "urban sprawl" spawned by the mushrooming mine camp.

Not so, Frisco! Community planners, backed by solid investment dollars, laid out an organized townsite, based on economic growth projections more solid than the glint of gold in a mountain streambed. As a transportation crossroads, first for wagon and stagecoach travel and ultimately for the railroad, Frisco's future looked secure. The hope of mineral riches, frosting on the town developers' cake, soon emerged as dazzling reality, with a chain of gold and silver strikes in the nearby Gore and Ten Mile ranges. Frisco, alone among Summit's communities, began as a new town investment by nineteenth century American capitalists—not as a frenzied swarming camp, called into being by a prospector's exultant cry of "Gold!"

Frisco prospectors penetrated the Gore range via Eccles Pass with dozens of rich silver strikes by the early 1880s.

CHAPTER 2

Blue Ribbon Years

People poured into 1880s Frisco and the clamoring crowd put up buildings, discovered silver, jubilated over the railroad's arrival, demanded schools and celebrated in such a rowdy fashion that town fathers clamped down on the revelers with new laws. Frisco flourished in the early '80s, and cash registers along Main Street rang merrily.

Frisco business, thriving by 1881, boasted a variety of stores and services. An October, 1881 newspaper reported:

> Population is now 300, and Frisco is a supply point for 200-300 miners. There are 3 hotels [Frisco, Stafford's and Leyner], 3 supply houses [Scott, Evans and Charles Thompson], various saloons and a smithy [Baliff].

Frisco's two-year old postoffice stood in its crossroads position on three different postal routes in 1881. Along with the High Line from Georgetown, another daily mail carrier mounted difficult Argentine Pass (13,132 feet) from Georgetown to service Peru Creek towns of Decatur and Chihuahua before its Frisco stop. Mail also arrived via wagons and hacks from Breckenridge three times weekly. For juggling all these deliveries, William Jackson, postmaster, earned $13 annually.

Business growth swelled through 1885. V. J. Coyne had taken over Peter Leyner's popular Leyner House and spruced up the place, "adding new rooms, new bedding and papering," according to the *Montezuma Millrun.* "Frisco begins to look lovely, bright and neat."

With area mines engaged in a flurry of construction, Frisco's three supply stores enjoyed a smart trade. (In an era of false-front buildings, William Evans & Sons store stood an imposing two stories.) The enterprising merchants carried their goods to the consumer, who often chose remote locations. Jack (burro) or pony trains ran all summer to various mines and mine camps. J. S. Scott's trains serviced camps in the Gore Range, including Angels Camp at the

Red Peak mines, according to the *Rocky Mountain News*. Hikers traversing the trails from Frisco to Red Peak via 11,900-foot Eccles Pass today know the stamina required for this trek!

Frisco's late 1880s witnessed a business slowdown, prompted by an 1886 decline in silver prices from about $1.07 to $.91 per ounce, according to the August 21, 1886 *Montezuma Millrun*. On top of that, the entire U. S. experienced an economic slide in the late '80s. Frisco miners doubled their efforts, increasing volume to make up for the price drop. Silver miners all over the west did the same, probably contributing to the glut that helped bring about silver's devastating devaluation and the 1893 Silver Panic.

Frisco's roller coaster cycle of economic ups and downs saw its first downward roll. Businesses advertising in the 1888 *Colorado Business Directory* dropped to a limping assemblage of one saloon (Harry Britton's), one boarding house, one sawmill and one mine, Daniel Recen's prosperous Excelsior.

"Tip" Baliff had moved his blacksmith shop to Dillon. William Evan's grocery and Newne's wheelright shop had quickly followed, according to the 1888 *Colorado Business Directory*.

Some wags might attribute the town's economic sluggishness to the frigid 1887-88 winter, which made commercial trade as brisk as molasses in January. On December 21, 1887, for example, temperatures plummeted to -20 degrees before midnight, -30 at 2 a.m., -38 at 3 a.m. and -42 degrees at 4 a.m., according to Rev. Mark Fiester's *Blasted, Beloved Breckenridge*. When thermometers quit working, Frisco saloonkeepers examined their best rum to see if the purest of their stock had frozen.

Mining in the 1880s: A Discovery Decade

When Henry Learned discovered his pioneering Kitty Innes Mine near Frisco, he made 1881 *Denver Daily Tribune* news headlines. "It was on Royal Mountain, up the Ten Mile Creek, in the Kitty Innes Mine, that the lucky finder threw down his pick. After discovering the body of rich, glittering mineral, (he) sang the first stanza of the well-known song 'Rock of Ages, Cleft for Me'."

Learned's enthusiasm caught the imagination of hundreds of would-be miners, enough to double Frisco's population in a year. Silver, lead and gold assays backed up Learned's zeal, valued at $20 to $190 per ton, depending on the ore. Summit County entered the decade with an impressive $2.6 million production of gold, silver, lead, copper and zinc in 1881. (Readers should remember that dollar values can be multiplied by seven due to inflation and that gold traded at less than $20 per ounce.) The Denver papers hailed Frisco's lucrative future. "There are hundreds of good mines just waiting for some prospectors today," the *Tribune* advised. "Miners can get plenty of work in the camps at remunerative wages."

Prospectors first focused on the mountains just south and west of Frisco. Mt. Royal and the steep-cut walls of the Ten Mile Canyon were soon riddled with glory holes. The effort paid off. Mines in 1881 included the Frisco Discovery and Mining Company's tunnel, driven into stubborn Mt. Royal granite, the Royal Mountain Mining and Milling Company's 160-foot tunnel and silver strikes on Miners Creek.

Though the 1880-81 snows piled up deep drifts in a heavier-than-normal accumulation, gleeful miners worked right through the winter, making discoveries.

Frisco's earliest lode mine, the 1866-discovered Victoria, produced $10,000 in gold in 1880. The stunning Victoria Lode is located at the ruins of today's Masontown ghost camp site on Mt. Royal. A well-heeled Civil War officer, General Buford, put up a stamp mill to crush the Victoria's gold-rich ores. After costly investment and labor, General Buford one day simply vanished. (Locals maintain that he disappeared during mud season.) In 1872, Philadelphia and Georgetown investors built an ore reduction works rumored to cost a whopping $75,000 (big money in 1872). These developers renovated Buford's old mill and planned to add a refining process for gold and copper. Their goal: $800-$1,000 daily production. When the railroad arrived at Frisco in 1883, the Victoria's killer, ore transport costs, plummeted.

On a sunny, blue-sky winter day, observers of today can watch the homes, stores and offices of Frisco empty as locals head for the ski slopes. A century ago, the same phenomenon drew folks from Frisco's hotels, offices, saloons, postoffice and general stores to head for "them thar hills." But in those days the lure was gold, silver and lead. Practically every name linked to the mines mentioned here belongs to a Frisco businessman who wore two hats—one as hotel proprietor or town trustee, the other a prospector's battered wide-brim.

Postmaster William Jackson joined storekeeper J. S. Scott to mine at the Eighty One Lode on Wichita Mountain. Frisco House proprietor David C. Crowell mined with Dan Smith on Mt. Royal and the Recen brothers worked their claim nearby. C. C. Warren worked the Green Mountain Girl, Lone Star, Mammoth and Little Lottie. Patrick Hopkins located the Copper Queen. John H. Garrison, an original Frisco trustee, worked up Miners Creek on "Learned's Hill."

By 1882, miners had penetrated the rugged Gore Range, northwest of Frisco, where trails along north Ten Mile Creek or Meadow Creek provide access across a high pass to Buffalo Mountain and Red Peak. Eccles Pass, named for one of the prospecting members of the Eccles (Eckles) and Taylor partnership, beckoned Frisco's citizens into the silver-laced Wilkinson Mining District, an area "busy as a hive" by summer, 1882. The deep cleft between Buffalo Mountain and Red Peak abounded in silver. Prospectors scrambled all over the area discovering veins with a dazzling 300 to 21,000 ounces of silver per ore ton, according to the *Denver Daily News*, January 11, 1882.

Spotlight on Frisco

Located centrally among the Breckenridge, Montezuma and upper Ten Mile Canyon mining regions, Frisco snared a plum in 1882: The May 3 Summit County Mining Convention. A year later, in September, 1883, delegates from the National Mining Convention, meeting in Denver, selected Frisco as a mountain excursion site. Frisco preened for the chance to strut its stuff before an array of distinguished guests. The exposure spurred Frisco's mining growth.

Peter Leyner's 1879-built hotel served a dynamic crossroads town.

Merchants scrambled to present their best face. Crawford and Co. rushed to move their stock into their "magnificent store," the April 19, 1882 *Summit County Times* reported. Frank "Red Peak" Wolfe hurried to complete the town's first picket fence surrounding his residence. The Leyner Hotel hastened through its renovation. The Frisco Dramatic Association rehearsed a new play, "Conscience," which they planned to present to the public "in regal style."

Frisco laid out the welcome mat, even encouraging the ladies to attend the first festive meet:

> Let there be a full representation from all camps, and a full delegation of the fair sex. There are ample hotel accomodations for all. A grand play at the opera house is in the evening, and two halls for dancing, to conclude with a grand supper. No pain or expense will be spared to entertain all that may come. Arrangements have been made to run extra stages at half fare for the occasion.
>
> *Summit County Times,* April 19, 1882

National Mining Convention visitors, who enjoyed autumn's colorful show enroute to Frisco, were properly impressed with Summit County's citizens. A high-flown *Rocky Mountain News* commentator complimented residents this way: "The people, like the county, are of the better class, and more intelligent or enterprising are rarely seen."

Colorful Colorado Mountain Railways

Nineteenth century American railroading represented the best of our nation's energy, expansiveness and enthusiasm to meet a challenge. Nowhere was the challenge more crucial than in the high mountain passes of Colorado where steep inclines, tortuous curves and near-impregnable rocky terrain tested the determination and ingenuity of railroad developers.

Both the Denver, South Park & Pacific Railroad (DSP&P) and the Denver & Rio Grande Railway (D&RG), the two that served Frisco, overcame near-impossible odds to create colorful railroad history in Colorado. Both railroads turned to narrow gauge, the shorter track width—three feet rather than the standard four feet, eight inches— that allowed mountain railways to negotiate tight curves, cling to narrow cliffsides, pass through tight rock cuts and tunnels. Frisco received service from two railways, a move that satisfied the fierce competition of the South Park line toward the D&RG, but ultimately caused the former's financial ruin. The DSP&P, an 1870's-developed mountain branch of the Union Pacific, battled the Denver & Rio Grande, using both legal process and physical assault, for the right to run its narrow-gauge track side-by-side with the D&RG's in the tight Ten Mile canyon. The intense rivalry to capture the lucrative Leadville freight business may have ruined the Denver, South Park and Pacific, but it paid off for Frisco area miners. The districts' low grade ores proved costly to haul, because Frisco ores contained less precious metal per ton than areas like Kokomo, with a much higher silver content. Competition kept ore freight rates down.

Prior to the railroad's arrival, sure-footed pack animals, little burros and mules, formed a "narrow gauge" pack train to haul ore along the Ten Mile Canyon's tricky trails. Burros could tote 200 pounds of ore each, or a mule hauled 300 pounds. When these primitive freight trains arrived at level ground, their loads were transfered to lumbering ore wagons. Often, a Frisco teenage boy would land his first job running a burro train.

All this exhausting work would be a thing of the past for most Frisco miners when the railroad came. Spurs built directly to the mines would eliminate even the challenging short hauls.

No wonder then that Frisco residents reacted with joy to the news on January 1, 1881 that the D&RG had scaled Fremont Pass to reach the upper Ten Mile Canyon town of Robinson. The Frisco town board met September 21, 1881 to grant a right of way to the coming railroad. They selected a 40-foot wide strip between Main and Galena Streets, a straight shot through town just north of and parallel to Main Street. In a free-wheeling gesture, the trustees also threw in 20 acres for a depot and work area. The D&RG quickly set to grading, which included raising town streets to track level where the new track crossed. With that work complete in October, the railroad had only to build three bridges and lay track from Wheeler (today's Copper Mountain area). Local sawmills experienced a bonanza providing pine ties for the railway, 3,000 ties for every mile of track.

While sawmills denuded surrounding mountainsides, another railroad-related business flourished near Frisco. Hathaway's kilns, on the Denver, South Park & Pacific track near Rainbow Lake, made coke for both 1880s narrow-gauge steam locomotives and for area smelters, according to old-timers. John Hathaway and Joe Lampkin once owned and operated nearly 50 coke ovens near Ophir Mountain. A series of three or four of these ruined kilns remains along the railroad grade.

"At one time Ophir Mountain was almost completely logged out for the coke kilns that used to be at the foot of Ophir Mountain," reported longtime resident Harold Deming in a 1979 letter to the Frisco Historical Society. "All the new forest you see on Ophir is second growth lodgepole pine."

The town board's recorder, in a surge of optimism, expressed in the Frisco town minutes that the first train would arrive "in a few days." Actually, Denver & Rio Grande construction crews remained in the Canyon through June of 1882, finally reaching Frisco that summer and Dillon on December 7, 1882. A year later, in July, 1883, Frisco's second railroad, the Denver, South Park & Pacific steamed into town. An exuberant town board donated 11 blocks of the original town plat to the South Park "by unanimous vote," according to the Frisco town minutes, August 1, 1883. The board also gave the railroad the town square—again by unanimous vote.

While the town wooed the railroad and glad-handed with its representatives, a disgruntled Silas W. Nott viewed the overnight disintegration of his once-thriving stagecoach line. Since July, Summit County and Leadville passengers could ride the rails all the way to their destinations. Nott retained the contract to carry the U. S. mail, but finally relinquished it to the Denver & Rio Grande. The *Montezuma Millrun* editor, no diplomat, rejoiced:

> At last. S. W. Nott has thrown up the sponge and quit trying to haul passengers and the mail over Loveland Pass. Hereafter we will receive our Denver and Eastern mail via Pueblo and Leadville, and we hope we will receive more regularly if not quicker than before.
>
> *Montezuma Millrun*, November 18, 1882

Dashing Concord coaches and lumbering ore wagons grinding up the Ten Mile Canyon to Leadville became a thing of the past. The railroads stood ready to meet all transportation challenges. And challenges there were: The avalanche-prone Ten Mile Canyon regularly dumped on the railroad track, snarling train schedules and adding to the DSP&P Railroad's nickname "Damned Slow Pulling & Pretty Rough Riding." Spring runoff swelled streams and washed out bridges. Brakes failed on steep mountain pass descents causing runaway trains. Passengers faced boarding hazards, according to Kokomo's *Summit County Times'* undated report on Frisco's 1881 mayor:

> A serious accident happened to Maj. W. A. Mensch, of Frisco, while getting off the South Park train at Denver some few days since. In stepping from the train to the platform, the

steps being covered with snow and the night stormy, he slipped having his little girl in his arms; in his endeavor to save
her he received a severe contusion of the hip. He is now
confined to his room suffering severe pain and will hardly be
liable to get out for several weeks.

Railroad Sparks Ruckus

Awaiting the rails' inchworm arrival, the town board had plenty
of time to dive into a fracas over just where the D&RG would
terminate. If Frisco became the rail line's terminus town, then Frisco
should have the county seat. As the excitement reached a fever
pitch, the town board ordered the town clerk to cease selling lots
while Henry Learned, J. S. Scott and Judge Bennett negotiated with
the D&RG, offering concessions to entice the railway to choose
Frisco as the terminus of its Blue River Branch.

Meanwhile locals jacked up the prices on their property, hoping
to make a killing when real estate values skyrocketed upon arrival
of the rail. Even the January 1, 1882 *Rocky Mountain News* prepond-
erated on this "great augmentation" in the value of Frisco's property.

The brouhaha over the county seat location erupted because both
Frisco and Dillon anticipated railroad service and each wanted to
be the last town on the line. Snake River miners and merchants in
the bustling towns of Decatur, Chihuahua and Montezuma resented
the long and expensive stagecoach ride to the county seat at Breckenridge to accomplish county business. So did the upper Ten Mile
towns, Kokomo and Robinson. The trips meant a costly overnight
stay in Breckenridge and a loss of two days work. These areas
lobbied for county seat transfer. The *Montezuma Millrun* jumped
into a squabble between Dillon and Frisco as contenders for a possible county seat relocation and supported Frisco. The centrally-
located town had, after all, set aside land to donate for county
buildings. The *Millrun's* fervent and unswerving support lasted until
an unconcerned Rio Grande Railway pushed past Frisco to make
Dillon the terminus of its line. Then the *Millrun* changed its tune.

An "Old Settler" from Frisco, possibly Henry Learned, wrote a
letter to the *Montezuma Millrun*, published October 21, 1883. The
writer scoffed at *Summit County Journal* editor Jonathan Fincher, who
dismissed Frisco as "out in the woods:"

> Frisco holds the key to the great Ten Mile Canyon and to
> the heavy mineral producing camps of Recen, Kokomo and
> Robinson, all of which have a world wide fame... That a

stranger could drive through the beautiful streets of Frisco and not know there was such a town, would be because he was blind, full of bug juice, or a candidate for a lunatic asylum...
OLD SETTLER

In the end, Dillon received 1,011 county seat votes in the November, 1882 elections. Frisco tallied only 285 and Breckenridge 832. Since the law required a two thirds majority vote, Breckenridge retained the county seat.

Frisco's Elegant Eighties

After a grim week in a damp, dark mine tunnel, with its year-round 55-degree temperature, miners jumped at the chance to throw down a pick axe and climb out of hobnailed boots for a Saturday night spree. Frisco's earliest social life took place when miners would "belly up to the bar" at B. B. Babcock's, Morrow's or Isador Smith's saloon. If things got rowdy, well, "the boys" would be boys. But Frisco night life had its cultural side as well. When more ladies joined their husbands in the emerging town, entertainment became highbrow. As early as 1880 a newspaper reported, "A grand ball

Denver & Rio Grande track took straight-arrow route through Frisco along alley between Main Street and Galena.

was given at the Frisco House a few evenings since."

Frisco celebrated Christmas, 1882 with a holiday dance advertised in the December 16 *Montezuma Millrun:* "Grand Hop, December 23rd, at the Frisco House, Game and Trout supper served up. Tickets: Lady and Gentleman, $2.00. Music by Prof. Hutton's band." "Frisky Friscoans fling fluttering feminity fast and furious tonight at the dance at the Clintons," the March 1, 1882 Summit County Journal trilled.

The *Journal* referred to a truly auspicious event: The opening of Frisco's new Graff Opera Hall and the drama troupe's debut with two offerings, "A Happy Pair," a Comedietta in one act and "Turn Him Out," a farce. Mr. and Mrs. J. J. Clinton celebrated the performance by hosting a soiree following. All of Frisco danced that night, as well as party goers from Kokomo, Ten Mile, Wheeler, Dillon, Braddock and Boreas. The crowd spilled out of the opera house into the spacious Frisco Hotel dining hall. Breckenridge alone "furnished upwards of forty couples," the *Journal* reported.

Mrs. Clinton lent her energies to the new Frisco Dramatic Association, the troupe that performed "Conscience" for the county Mining Convention. The *Journal* ran this report on February 27, 1882:

> We "Friscoans" still live and are full of ambition, life and energy. The latest novelty is an opera house... a large hall has been transformed into one of the nobbiest halls in the mountains... Several plays will be brought out in a short time by the Frisco Dramatic Association; we have some artists, residents of Frisco, that are not unknown upon the stage.

"All That Glitters Is Not Gold," an offering appropriate for its mining-oriented audience, opened at the Graff Opera Hall on October 30, 1882, according to the *Dillon Enterprise.* Admission to the comic drama in two acts—50 cents.

The man behind all this theatrical fun was A. C. Graff, a Breckenridge gold rush '59er and then an 1878 settler and mine discoverer at Kokomo, located just below Fremont Pass. In 1879, Kokomo stood unique among Summit's mine communities. The town had a fine brass band. Professor Graff, musical director, took the splendiferous musical group to social affairs around the county. After Kokomo burned, Graff moved to Frisco and opened his opera house February 29, 1882. An astute businessman as well as musical maestro, Graff had developed a profitable cattle business before moving to Kokomo where he opened an ore smelter. Graff & McNair's smelter served hundreds of upper Ten Mile Canyon mines. Graff resumed his cattle business in Frisco and also held the office of mayor. Around 1887, he moved his two-story opera house building to Dillon, where it still stands as the Three Rivers Rebekah Lodge and D & L Printing.

Drama and fancy dress balls lent a cultured polish to Frisco's social scene. But the early western mine town's civilized veneer could scratch easily. Frisco's seamy side, the low life evidenced in drunken saloon brawls, red light houses and six gun duels, sometimes erupted in bloodshed. A brutal barroom murder occurred on October 20, 1881 when James McWalters was bludgeoned and stabbed in the culmination of a disagreement over a card game and ethnic superiority.

McWalters, a British bartender at Morrow's Saloon, finished his shift at 9:15 and headed for Isador Smith's place, where he got into a card game and quaffed undetermined amounts of whiskey and blackberry brandy, the November 5, 1881 *Colorado Weekly Republican* reported. McWalters, accused of cheating, argued with gamesters James Driscoll and Patrick Hopkins, bringing into question the quality of the pair's Irish heritage.

McWalters retreated to Morrow's. Driscoll and Hopkins, tipsy enough to push their luck, strolled into Morrow's for a nightcap. A dispute over change for a drink charge caused McWalters to erupt in a barrage of obscene language and go for the saloon's rifle above the bar. Driscoll grabbed the gun and struck McWalters a cruel blow to the head with its butt. A knife finished the argument—and McWalters.

Police Justice Henry Learned directed the inquest, held at the scene of the crime over two and one half days. Witnesses testified before a six-man jury. Jury duty demanded a strong stomach, because, according to Anne K. and Don English's research paper "The Successful Miner," "during the entire time the body of the deceased was stretched out on the floor..."

Yankee Doodle Gets Drenched

Young America, intensely patriotic, paraded its best orators, orchestras, and its brightest stars and stripes for July 4, Independence Day. In Frisco, the weather had its own notion of "independence." In 1881, planners organized the celebration to a T, with afternoon races and games at a nearby lake to follow a morning of patriotic music and stirring speeches. The only problem lay in the fact that cloudbursts usually occur on summer afternoons in the Colorado mountains, beginning around July. When the band and a happy crowd of citizens repaired to the lake to watch the athletes who had trained for the races, "the rains began to fall, almost in torrents, making everthing an utter impossibility."

The *Breckenridge Daily Journal's* July 5, 1881 report capsuled Frisco's morning festivities, which took place under sunny blue skies, but indoors:

> ...the speaking and performances were held in Mr. Crowell's spacious hall in the Frisco Hotel. The music furnished by our band and Glee Club was excellent and for the short time in which Prof. Wagner had been drilling, the boys all did extremely well. The Declaration of Independence was read by Mayor W. A. Mensch owing to the unavoidable absence of J. P. Nicks. The oration by General C. C. Royce was superb in every particular... One of the most amusing features of the day was a humerous [sic] poem composed and read by Mr. Ferguson, who by the way is the most fertile genius in the camp...

Winter fun did not include skiing in the 1880s. Some Colorado towns, such as Crested Butte, closed their school on sunny winter days for downhill ski races. But not Frisco. Skis (called snowshoes) measured 12 feet long and four inches wide, weighing in at 15 pounds. Steering, a term used loosely here, was accomplished by wielding a long heavy pole, also dragged for stopping. One old timer responded to the author's question, "Could you turn on those things?" with "Sure, you could turn, but the skis never would." The miners used skis to travel to their snug tunnels where many worked the winter months through.

Sleighing, however, ranked high in 1880s Frisco. One resident pronounced the sport fine enough to lure travelers up from Denver to share the fun:

> There is splendid sleighing... it is worth the cost of the trip from Denver by way of Georgetown to enjoy such fine sleighing and having such a fine view of the snowclad peaks. We have been having splendid weather for a long time with only an occasional storm. To pass away the time pleasantly, the Frisco and Dillon folks meet quite often and wind up with a grand ball.
>
> *Rocky Mountain News*, January 11, 1882

Frisco Lays Down a Limp Law

While nearby towns like Montezuma cracked down on miscreants with stiff fines for drunks, gamblers and madams, Frisco saw a chance to pad its own pocketbook by licensing local vice. In March, 1883 the town first required liquor licenses (fee: $50 for six months) to gain some control of local revelers. But the town's indulgent policy toward tipplers always looked the other way. The town also cracked a whip of limp spaghetti at gamblers. The town board passed an ordinance declaring all pool, bagatelle and other gaming tables must be licensed at $5 per year. (This included bowling alleys.) Mayor Learned and the six-member board clapped their hands over their ears as the hurdy gurdy racket of dance hall music poured into the town streets and resolved to tax the bawdy establishments $10 per month. Then they turned a stern gaze on Frisco's soiled doves. In September, 1883, the trustees proclaimed, "The marshall is instructed to collect from all female frequenters, or inmates of Dance Halls, Saloons or any house known to be kept for the purpose of Assignations (prostitution) the sum of Five (5) Dollars per month." Every month the town marshall had the inglorious task of knocking on the Madam's door to collect his $5. (In Breckenridge, the shady ladies paraded into the town hall monthly to pay their proper fees. Breckenridge, too, legalized prostitution!) Licensing the world's oldest profession paid off for Frisco: 1884 town coffers bulged to a heady $1,000.

Town Patent Peekaboo

In 1882 the town fathers moved to secure a U. S. patent on the Frisco townsite. This simple action began a bureaucratic snafu (situation normal, all fouled up) unmatched in the annals of Summit small town government. The patent application process took almost a century to complete!

Board members bartered in March to hire Summit County Judge William A. Guyselman and attorney A. D. Bullis to secure the patent. The two gentlemen agreed to accept real estate, three town lots each, as payment for their services. Patent paperwork sailed along smoothly at first. Mayor Learned on August 18, 1882 had forwarded all patent papers to the Federal Land Office. In September, he presented a Certificate of Patent to the board. But by year's end, a letter from the Land Office commented on "some informality relative to granting of a patent for the Town of Frisco." Finally on February 26, 1885, President Chester A. Arthur signed the delayed document, granting the townsite land. The town board moved with the alacrity of an inchworm to record the patent, backpedaling until 1892, when Trustee John William Thomas finally dispatched it to Breckenridge. However, Thomas neglected to pay the recording fee. Seven years

27

later, in 1899, the town board received a bill from the Summit County Clerk and Recorder for that very past-due $5. Again the board managed to overlook payment. The document disappeared. In 1924, an efficient county clerk mailed the patent certificate copy to longtime 1900s Frisco postmaster, Louis A. Wildhack, who put it with his personal papers. More than 50 years later, in 1979, his son, William A. Wildhack found the nearly 100-year old but not-yet-official town patent among yellowed documents undisturbed for years. A delighted modern-day town board paid the recording fee and Frisco finally owned its own land. Unfortunately, any gold or silver strikes made by property owners excavating for homes or condominiums remain the property of Uncle Sam.

Jailbirds and Firefighters

Following that first move toward securing a town patent, the town board faced annual April elections. B. B. Babcock stepped

Captain
Henry Learned
1819-1903

Captain Henry Learned, who selected Frisco's site and named the area in the 1870s, stands out as the single most dedicated public servant in Frisco's history. The former federal district officer and Indian agent first arrived in Frisco at age 56. He never yielded to the temptation to retire to his rocking chair and let others take the town reins. Instead, Learned remained in public positions until months before his 1903 death at age 84.

A man of maturity, Captain Learned possessed the expertise to represent town investors during Frisco's initial development down as mayor.

New trustees immediately turned to a new task: Frisco needed a caliboose. Not only had the town marshall no badge, he had nowhere to house the criminals, neer-do-wells and rifraff he had the luck to nab. (The lawman drew a $4 bonus for each arrest.) In 1881, the town erected the Frisco jailhouse, preserved in the Frisco Historic Park today. The caliboose, constructed with old-fashioned square nails that disappeared from use after the early '80s, crimped the style of many an early day malefactor.

Nowhere did community pride focus more fiercely than on the early-day fire departments. Their proud dress uniforms, with brass buttons polished to a shine, appeared in July 4th parades and town celebrations. Firefighting ranked as serious business in the 1880s western mine town, for the progression of a typical town matured over years from log to frame to stone or masonry structures. In the

in 1879. Learned promoted the new community, encouraging its first townsfolk to settle and to build the sawmill, hotel, saloon, store, feed stable and corral under construction in spring, 1879.

The *Colorado Consistory News*, May-June, 1920, reported Learned's membership in the Masons. This provides a reason for Learned's friendliness with Henry Recen, also a Mason and builder of the stone foundation for Kokomo's 1880 Masonic Hall.

Henry and Hattie Learned sold newspapers and periodicals, plus running the postal station, in their 1885 grocery-notions store during Learned's first six-year stint as Frisco postmaster, 1883-89. (Learned again served as 1900-1902 postmaster.) Besides managing his Kitty Innes Mine, Learned held office as 1885 mayor and justice of the peace. He had helped organize Frisco's 1882-founded school as school district board secretary, and served many terms on the town board. Later, in 1890-91, the 71-year old Learned became Summit County coroner.

During Frisco's darkest years, the post-Silver Panic 1890s, Henry Learned held on to the town government when other elected officials neglected their posts. A quarter-century of loyal leadership in the town he helped found secures Captain Henry Learned's place as a Frisco pioneer.

1880s, log and wood frame construction prevailed. Every major Summit County town except Frisco and the upper Ten Mile Canyon's Robinson, had their main streets, and in some cases, the entire town, wiped out by fire.

During the 1882 county seat competition, Frisco had boasted its ability to quench fires in buildings of any height. In 1883, the town board instructed Frisco Fire Department Chief Engineer Frank Wolfe to upgrade an already praiseworthy department. The town bought poles with hook and chain, 24 buckets (for bucket brigades from water source to the fire) and ladders in sizes of 14, 18, 22 and 25-foot lengths, all stored in fire department headquarters, the town barn. Later, in 1889, the board resolved "to request the citizens to place a ladder on the side of their buildings and one from the side to the top... to help in fire protection..." Early Frisco photos show acquiescence of local residents. Trustees also asked citizens to keep a full water barrel handy. In summer, firefighting proved less challenging than during cold months when water barrels, town ditch and nearby streams froze.

The 1887 elections planted some new personalities at the town meeting table, among them Georgetown transplant, John W. Thomas, Frisco's new clerk, recorder and police chief, who as Main Street hotelman would create an impact on local history. Chauncey Carlisle Warren, new mayor, was a colorful local character. He came to Colorado in 1869, first to Central City and then to Silver Plume, where his wife, Mary, joined him to teach school. When road-builders hacked out 11,992-foot Loveland Pass in 1879, C. C. Warren opened a popular stage stop on the pass for rest and refreshment of travelers from Georgetown. The Warrens moved to Frisco after Silas Nott shut down his High Line stage. Warren's oldest son, Brad, won a post as 1887 town trustee beside his father. Rounding out the board were treasurer Charles Campbell, trustee and town marshall James S. Scott and trustees John Ledingham and Henry Learned.

Slate and Switch: Frisco School District Debuts

Census takers recorded Frisco resident J. P. Nick's occupation as school teacher, and it is probable that he took time out from prospecting to acquaint Frisco's smaller citizens with the 3 Rs. But their elders waited until summer, 1882 before taking steps to organize a local school district.

Henry Learned's ornate script flows across page one of the Frisco "Record of District Meetings" book. Learned detailed the July 24, 1882 meeting of legal voters "for the purpose of forming a school district and for the purpose of having the school in operation as soon as possible." Parents and others present voted unanimously to form the school district and elected the following as officers: William H. Evans, president; Henry Learned, secretary; Jasper Reynolds, treasurer.

Far-flung school district boundaries stretched from the Ten Mile range summit to Willow Creek (in the area of today's Willowbrook, north of Silverthorne), and from the Blue River and the Frisco-Dillon bridge (now under Lake Dillon waters) to the summit of the Gore range.

When the aspens shone yellow in September, school opened with nine boys and eight girls under the scholarly care of Mrs. Mann. Things went along swimmingly—for a couple of days. Then on September 11, trouble broke loose. Mrs. Mann complained to the school board about an unruly mischief-maker named George Reynolds. This incorrigible boy caused a class disturbance, refused to obey Mrs. Mann and "used vile language," according to Learned's report. "The trustees examined a number of the scholars and found the teacher not to blame", the records note. George's indignant father, school board treasurer Jasper Reynolds, immediately yanked the young rebel and also his two sisters from Mrs. Mann's classroom.

Recovered from its disruptive start, the school flourished for two years. Then Frisco's school fizzled between 1884 and 1887. In April, 1887, new resident John W. Thomas recorded a petition to county school superintendent Professor B. A. Arbogast to reorganize the school district. Voters met at Chauncey Warren's home on May 12, 1887 to affirm the reorganized district. Although women were allowed to vote in school board elections, only the following 11 men, Frisco community leaders, participated:

John Boyce	H. W. Hathaway	John W. Thomas
Harry Britton	John Ledingham	Chauncey Warren
Charles Campbell	J. McKenney	William F. Williams
Isaac Grewell	James Scott	

New board president James Scott moved with alacrity to provide both teacher and schoolhouse for Frisco's neglected scholars. He called a special meeting May 28, to engage Miss Willis to teach a three month session beginning June 1, for $60 per month. (Many early day schools held summer sessions because heavy winter snows threatened to swallow up young pedestrians. Summit never plowed its roads from the county's beginning to the 1930s.)

The board began in April, 1889 a quest for a suitable schoolhouse that ended with the handsome log schoolhouse that anchors the Frisco Historic Park today. A series of makeshift quarters were pressed into service. In April and May, 1889 school board members James Scott, Harry Britton and John W. Thomas investigated several proposals to buy a new school building. Their budget figure: Up to $75. On July 6, 1889, two months after school began, the board moved to buy "the present schoolhouse" from Peter Granith for a bargain $55.

Thirteen students in the 1880s cost the school district $29 each. The decade's teachers were Birdie Fincher and A. E. Jones, 1883; Miss Willis, 1887; Lillian Wise, 1888; and Miss Laughlin, 1889.

As the Frisco school district struggled through its initial years, its creators probably would have chuckled at the notion that a century later, the town would host a district superintendent's office, managing a near $5 million budget, and 1300 students in 1983. Frisco also houses the high school-junior high complex and a modern elementary school.

Popular dance pavilion at lovely Uneva Lake near Frisco provided a picture spot for Ten Mile Canyon party group.

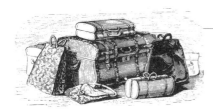

CHAPTER 3

Death Knell
for Frisco

If it's pneumonia, Mr. Probus said
Don't skid me off the Tenmile or I'll haunt
Your genteel casketry, old carmorant,
Old chronic end of evening, Dig my bed
Right in the boneyard at the valleyhead.
(Belle Turnbull, *The Tenmile Range*)

Everything went wrong for Frisco in the 1890s. While Brecken-ridge waltzed into an era of white gloves and wallpaper, plush private rail cars and 13-pound gold nuggets like "Tom's Baby," Frisco scraped the barrel's proverbial bottom.

Poor Henry Learned scurried to wear all the hats on the town board as trustees quit showing up for meetings. Somehow momentum petered out after an April, 1892 blizzard canceled the election, in predictable "Springtime in the Rockies" fashion. A snowbound D&RG failed to deliver election ballots. While an election did take place in May, the citizens managed to mandate the most lethargic group of loafers in Frisco's history. Twenty-three straight months elapsed without a meeting quorum. Only the clerk and recorder, the loyal Mr. Learned, showed up. Even he gave his last gasp in March, 1894 and not another town meeting took place till 1899.

An affront against Frisco's sporting element occurred in 1891 when the Colorado Saloon Law, enacted April 7, required that saloons close at midnight on weekdays and all day Sunday. Since the owner of Frisco's sole saloon, Harry Britton, always paid his liquor license fees (some did not), he probably obeyed the law, to the dismay of the drinking set.

While reeling from this blow, miners faced a much deadlier jolt, one that brought the Ten Mile Canyon, and its sister silver mining communities of Montezuma and Decatur, to their economic knees. In 1893, The U. S. Congress repealed the Sherman Silver Purchase Act. Silver's price dropped to almost half. The federal government had demonetized silver during its all-time peak production year and returned to exclusive use of the gold standard, a move that created ghost towns all over the West.

Frisco miners, and the merchants who depended on their trade, found themselves forced to leave the area or tighten their belts and try to hang on. Oddly enough, the miners themselves played a part in causing the Panic of 1893, by their ballooning output. Silver's biggest production year ever in the U. S. was 1892.

Not Gold Dust—Sawdust!

One industry that kept Frisco's 175 population alive was logging. Israel White worked up on aspen-dappled Meadow Creek with "two or three sawmills and five or six settings," an early day "History of Summit County" Summit Schools scrapbook maintains. John Safford, Shad Smith and a Mr. Guller worked in the wooded North Ten Mile Canyon with 20 or 30 settings. And Frisco for years had at least one sawmmill on Miners Creek. "Mr. Morgan and Mr. Win Shaw had sawmills" there, the scrapbook noted. Today, at the Miners Creek hiking path's upper trailhead, sawmill ruins remain to intrigue the curious.

The sawmill communities maintained a separate existence, the school scribes wrote:

> These lumber companies shipped lumber to Leadville, provided mines with the necessary timber, and made railroad ties. They usually continued their operations winter and summer, despite the long severe winters, and most of them employed forty and fifty men constantly. Living quarters were furnished near the mills and the life and activities around the sawmill camps may be compared to that of a small town...

Greed, carelessness and little awareness of environmental concerns in an era that sought "Progress," resulted in a rape of the virgin forest that would make today's watchful U. S. Forest Service rangers weep.

Frisco-born Harold "Chick" Deming in a letter to the Frisco Historical Society, explained that "almost all the canyons around Frisco had logging activity" and decried the timber harvesters' destruction.

> The early loggers were not concerned nor had they heard of the sustained yield concept of modern forestry and when they cut timber they cut only the best, but devastated the mountainsides getting it out. Forest fires were common, some

of them due to carelessness and some purposely set to get dry logs... Many of the pictures of the three peaks, Royal, Wichita and Chief show how bare the mountains were from indiscriminate logging.

Logging helped keep Frisco alive. Businesses failed and buildings fell into disrepair. But Peter Leyner's 1880-built Leyner Hotel, its roof caved in, gained new life during the funereal '90s, salvaged by dynamo newcomers, John and Jane Thomas, a Welsh couple who came to Frisco from Georgetown in 1887. Their daughter, Helen Elizabeth (Nellie) wrote a Thomas Family history years later:

> Frisco at this time was greatly in need of a hotel and as the old Layner's [*sic*] Hotel was being advertised for taxes, my father bought it and began repairing the building. It was in a deplorable condition... walls and roof open to weather. The hotel had been used for a stage coach stop, and also the barns which were located across the street or road. The hotel was built of logs and frame, and consisted of 11 rooms upstairs and 6 rooms and large cellar on first floor. After lots of hard work repairing it, the building became liveable. Mother ran "The Frisco Hotel," which it was now called, for many years...
>
> Pearl Garvin letter to the Frisco
> Historical Society, 1979, quoting Nellie Thomas Mogee

Bleak Frisco Main Street photo shows old Leyner Hotel. Welsh couple, John and Jane Thomas, revived historic lodge.

FRISCO!

Big Snow Winter, 1898-99

Summit's early winter snows are usually spare, despite the fervent prayers of today's ski area operators. But the county is almost always blessed by a holiday megadump, just in time to create a dazzling white Christmas.

Autumn, 1898 stretched long and balmy, lulling local residents into the irrational hope that winter's blasts might never come. On the night of November 17, sleepy residents, who stopped to peer outside before climbing upstairs with candle or lamp, noticed flakes tumbling from a cloudy sky. While they dreamed, snow poured in sheets. Frisco awoke to snow shoulder and chin high. Five feet of the white stuff fell before 9 a.m., November 28. But this proved to be only the opening number in a snowstorm extravaganza unparalleled in Frisco's history. Moisture-laden clouds unleashed snow almost nonstop every day from November 27, 1898 to February 20, 1899. Small children had to be watched, for snow rose above the first story to second story windows. People dug tunnels to their barns and walked in darkness to feed their animals in darkness. Older children emerged from upstairs windows to play their days away, as school remained closed. General stores ran out of snowshovels, grocery stores ran out of food, saloons ran out of liquor. "The snow was so deep, much of it as high as the telephone poles," recalled Frances Cherryholmes Nincehelser in a letter to the Frisco Historical Society. "People just tunneled through to various places. Where tunneling wasn't done, people walked on top of the snow with their snow shoes."

Frisco lay snowbound. Both the Colorado and Southern (C&S, formerly the DSP&P) and the Rio Grande railroads battled valiantly to keep track open and trains running, but both finally gave up. The angry storm king, Boreas, blew 20-foot drifts over track just cleared by the tough Leslie rotary snowplow on the C&S Boreas Pass route from Como to Breckenridge. At the Ten Mile Canyon town of Wheeler, Rio Grande cars froze into the snow and forced passengers to live there two or three weeks, eating foodstuffs probably enroute to Frisco. Finally, the men made skis from snow fence planks and skied to Leadville. Their feat made the *New York Times*, February 13, 1899. "Two prospectors on snowshoes arrived in Leadville today from Wheeler. It took them four days to make the trip of 14 miles." The *Times* recorded slides and drifts of 20 to 30 feet, sometimes two miles across the wagon road. "There is enough food at Wheeler and other towns around Kokomo, (Frisco) and Dillon to last 10 days with care but stock is suffering."

Snow blockaded the railroad for many weeks after this article, estimating 10 days food supply, appeared. Breckenridge, served by the C&S, remained sequestered for 79 days. The first train finally struggled through, with seven engines pushing the rotary snowplow, on April 24. How long snowbound Frisco waited for the D&RG to break through Fremont Pass and Ten Mile Canyon drifts is unknown. Frisco's neighbor, Dillon, managed to survive, due to the heroic efforts of stagecoach drivers who kept the Kremmling-Dillon stage line open and supplies moving throughout the blockbuster winter.

For Frisco, buried in white, the winter was a turning point. A tenacity born of the town's lean years drew residents together to share not only food supplies, but social life during a winter when miners could not work and storekeepers had little to sell. Pulling through that long winter together proved Frisco's last real hardship for more than a decade to come. For Frisco stood poised on the brink of an era of prosperity and growth unmatched in its history.

Mining: New Life in the '90s

Prosperity didn't appear to be in the cards in 1897 when 100 local placer and lode mines went on the sale block to cover back taxes. Among those advertised in the December 11, 1897 *Summit County Journal* were Daniel Recen's Excelsior Lode, at the Ten Mile Canyon's mouth (taxes due: $19.91); Mt. Royal's rich Victoria; Ophir Lodes ($2 due); the Surprise on Chief Mountain; the Warrior; and the Columbine.

While Frisco miners cried the blues in 1897, explosive progress marked the mining industry that year. Its shock waves would soon shake Frisco out of its doldrums.

The *Wonderland Quarterly*, one of Colonel J. H. Myers' newsletters, looked back on the '90s in a January, 1904 edition and summed up Frisco's mining status:

> When the miners of the Rocky Mountains could not make silver mining pay, they saw the necessity of digging deeper, until the gold zones should be reached... The wonderful advancement made in metallurgical processes [circa 1897] and the lessening of cost of supplies and transportation, together with the reduced cost of machinery, suddenly transformed the old silver camps into gold camps.

The prospectors who swarmed Frisco's mountains in 1879-97 scoured the peaks only for silver—when the area actually concealed a storehouse of gold.

Colonel Myers, who settled in Frisco in the 1890s, became a zealous proponent of "deep mining," relying on the excavation of long tunnels at sky-high cost, to reach the gold hidden by Mother Nature in the bowels of Frisco's granite peaks.

Myers hit Frisco like the runty, hawk-eyed, bewhiskered bombshell that he was, snaring a town clerk and recorder post in the April, 1899 elections. A promoter par excellence, he dove into an activity vital to the resurrection of Frisco's mining industry: Corporate organization and investment. The costly deep mining via tunnels that Myers proposed required huge dollar outlays. Driving one, two and three thousand feet into the rocky shoulders of the ancient Ten Mile Range demanded round-the-clock work crews, modern steam-driven drills, air compressors, power plants, and expensive cyanide process in mills. Corporate mining ventures, with many stockholders supplying capital, would finance development of legendary tunnels, like Colonel Myers' 7,000-foot King Solomon bore into Mt. Royal's western slope. And via the corporation, or the popular "syndicate," a promoter like Myers could make a nice living without ever losing his shirt.

Early day version of kids' 10-speed provided both pet and transport. Frisco's Main Street would soon bustle as mining's new day dawned.

Colonel
James Havens Myers

1844-1924

Author, mining expert, newspaper editor, savvy promoter, crusader, Frisco town official and longtime resident, Colonel James H. Myers left his spirited stamp on the town's history. He stormed into Frisco in the late '90s, armed with an unswerving resolve to prove his deep mining theory. The power of this conviction transformed Frisco from a played-out silver town to a thriving gold district. Col. Myers' magnetism drew untold amounts of investment dollars to Frisco's mines, a big shot of adrenalin to its anemic economy. And the concrete evidence of this man's visionary drive, the big mine dumps that mark tunnels up to 7,000 feet into Ten Mile Canyon mountain walls, demonstrate that Myers' dream became an undeniable reality.

This well-born son of a wealthy Virginia planter and scholar came to the Rocky Mountains to seek gold when Northern armies destroyed his home and inheritance during the Civil War. He married his wife, Louise, enroute, and formed his King Solomon Mining Syndicate upon arrival in Colorado in the 1860s. As early as the 1880s, he was capturing the imaginations—and the investment dollars—of affluent businessmen with his zeal for the promising Crysolite Mine near old Chihuahua.

He knew how to use newspaper editors, throwing out quotable one-liners as tantalizing as the ore samples he laid on their desks. During his years in Frisco, he fired a regular volley of news releases, letters to the editor and on-the-scene reports to the *Summit County Journal* and *Breckenridge Bulletin* that established himself as mining's local kingpin and Frisco as the county's hottest mining item.

Tough as a bantam rooster—and not much bigger—Myers knew how to duck when his detractors threw stones, and how to scramble to the top of the resulting heap when they were done. The pragmatist Colonel, who screamed at the first hint of dishonesty or fraud in others, left a trail of suspicious deals scattered behind him in his push to "get the job done." For example, a promotional prospectus on Myers' Mint Mine near Frisco pictured Gold Run Gulch's dazzling Jessie Mine on its frontispiece. The text claimed that the two properties were a pair—quite a departure from the truth.

"He never gave up, regardless of what happened," the *Summit County Journal* stated years after Myers death in 1924, "Summit County never had a better booster."

Almost overnight, Frisco's mines sprang back to vibrant new life. Partners Wyborg & Ault had purchased Dan Recen's Excelsior. Right away, Ault and Ohio printing ink magnate Frank Wyborg constructed and equipped an ore concentration mill. Developers then installed Frisco's first electric power at the Excelsior by damming nearby North Ten Mile Creek to create a reservoir. From the reservoir, workers rechanneled water to power a wheel to provide "several hundred horsepower" which created electricity to power the mine, mill and neighboring mines as well.

The Excelsior's walloping $50,000 development had progressed to the point in September, 1899 when the mine stood ready to "start its compressor and air drills" and hire a "large force" of miners, the September 22, *Breckenridge Bulletin* article announced. By 1901, the winter work crew alone numbered 15, according to the April 18 *Denver Times*.

Cash poured into Frisco-area mines produced an immediate payback. By year's end, all the mines within one mile of Frisco produced returns ranging from $10 to $300 per ore ton of gold, the December 31, 1899 *Denver Times* reported. The *Breckenridge Bulletin* also capsuled the year with a cheerful declaration—"the camp's future is no longer problematical!"

Don't Wake Me

Frisco town government, slumbering in coma, jerked awake when miners' hobnail boots clumped through town streets once more. New families also arrived, including the C. O. Linquists who opened a Main Street hotel, today's Frisco Lodge. Voters in 1899 chose the only ticket available that April, the Republican. Among those elected were Mayor Harry Britton and Colonel James H. Myers, clerk and recorder. Myers' first job: To search cobwebby town records and determine who had neglected to make second and final payments on lots purchased with money down in 1882. Forfeited lots, 39 in all, went on the block May 24, 1899, town minutes reveal. The town board duly noted that half of each forfeited lot belonged to the South Park (reorganized as Colorado and Southern) railroad, as per the board's expansive 1883 agreement.

The school board snapped up a smart bargain as part of the real estate sale. For $1, the school district bought a lot and a building on June 13, 1899. The property, lot 7 in Frisco block 8, was located where the Moose Jaw Restaurant is today.

Voters elected Elisha D. Deming, a name to appear in Frisco records over many decades, as school board president on May 5,

1890. By 1892, District No. 9 introduced a nine-month school term. Special meeting minutes from March 16 said: "It was resolved to keep school open nine months to commence April 3 and end December 29, with three weeks vacation in August, vacation to begin August 5 and end August 24."

For the first time in the 1890's women, who had the right to vote in school elections and hold district offices, exercised their privileges and participated. Among them: Eugenia (Mrs. Harry) Britton, Jane Thomas and Mrs. Linquist. The ladies bought a new school flag, 12 by 6 ½ feet for $6.90 and decided to order more books, "principally of the poets," both in 1899. John D. Hynderliter, another prominent Friscoan, first served on the board, as president, in 1897.

Schoolteachers in the 1890s

Miss V. Williams	1891
Mrs. Sue D. Fryer	1892
Miss V. Williams	1893-95
Miss Ruth Hamilton	1896-97
Miss Marguerite Detwieler	1898
Mrs. Louisa Gould	1899
Salaries: $50-60 per month, plus	
$20 monthly extra for janitorial fees	

Frisco celebrated a banner year by building a new Town Hall, slated for completion in time for July 4 festivities. In familiar mountain fashion, construction workers fell behind schedule and delivered a finished building in time for another holiday: Christmas, 1899. "All coming to the ball may count on a good time," the December 16 *Breckenridge Bulletin* advised. "A splendid supper will be served by the ladies." This old town hall still stands on Main Street today, at Third Street, a brown frame building. Its floor bears the imprint of decades of Friscoans' dancing feet.

An early day picnic in the pines gathered fun lovers of all ages for a summer Sunday's balmy pleasures. *Recen Family photo.*

Passenger awaits tardy train along twin track of D&RG and C&S. Rio Grande's "box car" depot stands in rear. C&S' tiny station sidelined Mt. Royal.

CHAPTER 4

Frisco's Heyday

Frisco danced out of the doldrums of its not-so-gay '90s and partied its way through the next decade. Townspeople had a reason to celebrate. The 1900s brought huge cash investments to Frisco's mines, a flood of new residents, business prosperity, electric power and telephone service, plus a fine new schoolhouse to an up-and-coming Frisco. Its residents kicked up their high-buttoned heels in joy.

The 1899-completed town hall served as the scene of dances and parties fondly remembered by longtime residents. Frisco tapped a lively foot through good years and bad to musicians such as 1900 violinists George Lottage, Frank Barkalow and Lars Matson (brother of Mrs. Henry Recen, 1870s pioneer). S. H. Bigelow played the Frisco Amusement Club's proud new piano. Square dance callers joined this musical foursome for a "Masquerade Ball," April 14, 1900, attended by 50 happy guests. Unmasking at midnight was usually followed by a fancy supper. Then dancers tripped the light fantastic till daylight.

Balls became an excellent way to raise cash for worthy causes. And no cause stood more worthy in Frisco's eyes than its baseball team. Fierce rivalry among neighboring towns fostered an equally fierce pride in the home team. In 1906, the June 6 *Bulletin* announced: "The Frisco Ball Team will serve a dance and supper at that place the evening of the 12th." The team had wound up its last season walloping Breckenridge 17-4 in September, 1905 and feeling ran high for the new season. The old baseball field, fitted with backstop nets by the town fathers, lay at Frisco's east end, where today's U.P.L. lumber outlet stands.

A double Independence Day victory in Breckenridge prompted the 12 Frisco baseball team members and their chunky mascot, Mayor Hart's little son, to pose for a victory photograph in 1909. The *Breckenridge Bulletin's* July 31, 1909 Frisco edition, carried the picture and the game results: "On Sunday, July 4, at Breckenridge,

Frisco defeated Montezuma by a score of 5-4. On the same grounds the following day, Breckenridge lost to Frisco in a hotly contested game. Score, Frisco 5, Breckenridge 2." Sil Bernard pitched the Frisco victory, aided by teammate Jack Haley who "landed the ball up among the pines over the center's head."

High hilarity marked Frisco's summer fun, especially at the big party-picnics. This local picnic gathered the area's Swedish residents for a merry time:

A jolly picnic party from Frisco and Dickey selected a se-cluded but none the less beautiful spot between two points, where they felt safer in making all the noise that seemed pos-sible to find penned up in a crowd of its size.

Of course the men folks in the party came well supplied with Swedish punch, etc., etc., etc.—and cigars enough to start a drug store on the premises, and they were not long in appointing a druggist to pass 'em around again and see to it that every ailment of whatever nature was promptly allayed with one of the many remedies in stock.

After the appetites of the merrymakers were sharpened by the brisk mountain air and a long wait in between meals, and music, singing, and hilarious noise were indulged in for several hours, the ladies made a spread on the ground which, judging from the bounteous supply of everything, looked as if it had grown on the surrounding trees and could be had for the picking. About five gallons of milk, etc., etc., etc. (water not included in the etc.'s) was used to wash down the good things and when the crowd disbanded late in the day, everyone was brim full of brotherly love for everybody else in the crowd. Present were Mrs. Williams (mother of the crowd), and Miss Avelin Hedenskog of Denver; Mr. W. F. Rathbone (the drug-gist) wife and children of Pine Grove; Mr. and Mrs. Con Ecklund (the two noisiest in the crowd) of Frisco; Miss Anna Flannigan (Matsson's best girl) of Dickey; L. A. Wildhack (he that broke seven plates of his camera on the crowd, after which he gave up in despair); Lars Matsson (the jolly fiddler), Eric Halben (he that wore the pair of borrowed leather lined riding pants the night before), Ed Skogsberg (the hard single- or double-handed hitter), Knute Hillstone (not Millstone), Henry Recen (ye oldest resident of Summit County and locator of the town of Recen), Mrs. Linquist and daughters Anna and Leda (the trio of the Linquist Hotel fame), all of Frisco; Andy

and Ole Westlund (from over the range) of Como, and Alfred
Johnson (the only temperance man in the crowd) of Dickey.
Breckenridge Bulletin, August 25, 1900

Cash Registers Ring

Turn of the century Frisco business life sparkled with the era's
excitement. Colonel James H. Myers and his string of investor properties—by 1904 every known mining claim on the Ten Mile Canyon
east wall, from the King Solomon five miles south to Wonderland
near Wheeler—paraded excursion groups of potential Eastern investors past his glittering mines, and past Frisco's eager business communities. One thriving from the influx was John and Jane Thomas'
Thomas Hotel, the 1879-founded Leyner Hotel, an imposing two-
story building with first- and second-story balconies. The building,
with a livery out back, stood just west of the present Frisco Lodge.
Its neighbor, the Frisco Hotel, belonged to the prominent Linquist
Family. The building remains at Fourth Avenue and Main Street as
the Frisco Lodge. In August, 1900, the Linquists hurried to complete
a 12-room addition to accommodate railroad excursionists. The
Southern Hotel, with S. H. Wood as its first proprietor and Con
Ecklund its popular second owner-manager, also housed the constant flow of prospective investors hosted by Colonel Myers, his
jovial son J. H. "Dimp" Myers, Jr. and daughter Mattie Myers. John
Hays also provided lodgings in his boardinghouse, according to the
1900 *Colorado Business Directory*.

Henry Learned's wife, Hattie, ran a 1900s general merchandise
store. Peter Prestrud, whose grandson still lives in Summit County
today, advertised his general store weekly in Dillon's *Blue Valley
Times*. The Frisco Supply Store, Nils Nilander, prop., offered "a full
line of Eatables, Fresh and Salt Meats, Fruits, Vegetables, Butter,
Poultry, Eggs, Fish and Game," according to his 1900 *Breckenridge
Bulletin* ad. Frisco residents had learned to live on salt pork, beans
and an occasional taste of fresh duck or venison in winter. When
Nils Nilander died from injuries sustained during a runaway of his
grocery delivery wagon team, Frisco mourned the man and his
merchandise.

Frisco's watering holes experienced a wild surge in business in
the mining heyday 1900s. Longtime resident Howard Giberson remembered his father, Wilbert Giberson, telling him Frisco had eight
saloons, although estimates run as high as 19 dancehalls and 20
saloons, a figure given writer Helen Rich by Mrs. Blundell, who
added that "no decent woman was allowed on the steet without an

escort." In the 1900s, saloonkeepers included J. Deming, licensed July 11, 1903; Riley & Rouse (Riley also served as marshall in 1904-05); Sheldon and Staley, licensed 1905 (Staley a freighter, served as town trustee in 1902); Deaner and Osborne (they took over Rouse & Levene, which had been Riley & Rouse); Robert D. Wiley; and Oliver Swanson (Swanson, a miner, hit a nine inch streak of 40-ounce per-ton gold at his Treasure Vault Mine the year his saloon opened).

Meanwhile, the town board busied itself with essentials like its September 7, 1901 ordinance declaring that "All livestock is to be kept off the streets at night." (Residents found sleep rather fleeting when a burro brayed into the bedroom window or when lowing cattle grazed on the moonlit lawn.)

"Operator. May I Help You?"

With livestock curfewed, Frisco trustees turned to negotiation for the town's first utilities. Frisco received telephone service after the turn of the century, a thoroughly modern amenity indeed! Frisco had its own telephone exchange in 1904 and a local agent representing Colorado Telephone, F. H. Labbo.

Envied electric lights burned outside town by 1899 at the Excelsior Mine and its little log camp, and by 1905 at the Canyon's North American and Mary Verna Mines. But Frisco still depended on gas lamps, kerosene and candles.

In 1907, when the Central Colorado Power Company finally plugged Frisco in, the new line carried more than 100,000 volts. Frisco had jumped from zero to 550 volts of electricity when the temporary power line from Leadville reached completion. Then the Shoshone Dam in the Colorado River's Glenwood Canyon went into operation, and the Frisco line's 100,000-plus volts made it the most powerful voltage generated for long distance use in the world, according to 1909 Frisco mayor J. Percy Hart, in the July 31, 1909 *Breckenridge Bulletin*, Frisco Edition.

"Nothing has done more to revive interest in mining than the building of the high voltage power line into the Frisco district by the General Colorado Power Company," Hart wrote. "Properties abandoned years ago on account of the great cost of fuel can now be operated by electric power."

Old timers say that Chinese laborers worked in the Frisco power plant around 1907. Years later curiosity over a set of dome-shaped structures that locals labeled "the Chinese huts" stirred memories. One resident remembered a Chinese cook coming into Frisco from the Ten Mile Canyon to buy groceries. Frisco's Marie Zdechlik un-

Jane Thomas
1853-1937

Photo courtesy Jim Yust

Frisco's best-loved lady ever arrived in 1887, a pint-sized powerhouse who mothered orphans, broke up barroom brawls, delivered babies, nursed the sick and stole the heart of early-day Frisco.

The Welsh-born woman waded through deep snows one moonless winter night to Masontown to aid a pregnant mother in labor. Mrs. Thomas single-handedly delivered twins that cold night on Mt. Royal.

Both the Thomases and the Linquists operated hotels on Main Street. Mrs. Linquist died when her baby daughter, Ida, was less than two years old. But tiny Mrs. Thomas was big enough for this sad situation. Ida Linquist Murphy wrote:

> Darling Mrs. Thomas. She mothered us girls after we lost our mother... My Dad hired women to come help run the hotel and care for us girls. They apparently didn't like caring for a baby. That was left to my sisters who took me with them wherever—I had some narrow escapes when they were playing; one a deep cut just missing my eye. Mrs. Thomas took care of it. Another time I got a whistle stuck in my throat. My Dad was running to the only phone in the town to call a doctor in Dillon who would have to come with horse and buggy. Before my Dad could reach the telephone Mrs. Thomas had grabbed me by the heels and shook me. Out came the whistle. I loved her.

Jane Thomas and her husband, John, had both emigrated from Wales and met in silver-studded Georgetown, Colorado. The couple married there in 1880. Their son, William John, was born in 1882 and the family had another son, Walter, along with a daughter, Helen Elizabeth, called Nell. In 1887, the Thomases moved to Frisco to homestead a ranch and manage Leyner's old lodging, renamed the Thomas Hotel. Jane ran the hotel and John supervised a stagecoach station and livery stables. John Thomas died in 1900, but the Thomas Hotel thrived, becoming Frisco's social center.

The Thomas children attended school in Frisco's old schoolhouse. Bill Thomas began working driving ore-laden burro trains for area mines at age 11. He later conducted tours of the King Solomon Mine. He earned enough to buy himself a sporty conveyance in October, 1901 when the *Breckenridge Bulletin* teased, "Thomas is sporting a fine new buggy. It is believed that he will have to get a 5th wheel... to make it strong enough to bear up all the girls who will want to test the springs. Now girls, look pretty."

Bill and his brother, Walter, lived on the Thomas dairy ranch in later years. The sight of Bill walking his cows to a pasture near Frisco became familiar to townsfolk. He married Minnie Dusing, a lady beloved by Frisco's children, and their colorful life together provided Frisco with plenty of rich conversation. Bill's ranch became the scene of winter ski parties after Minnie discovered the exhilarating sport. Minnie, later injured by ice falling from a roof one spring, lived in Breckenridge for years in the Prize Box building, her home. Bill's sister, Nell, married rancher Dan Mogee and lived near Dickey.

Jane Thomas died at Bill's ranch in June, 1937 at 84 years. Her son, Walter, passed away in the mid-'30s and Bill died in 1952.

Jane Thomas was buried in the Frisco cemetery. Wib Giberson, Ed Stuard, Dimp Myers, Charles Turner, Henry Recen and Bob Deming acted as pallbearers at this much-loved lady's funeral.

earthed a milk glass bottle containing a Chinese opium pipe from her driveway. The tiny pipe, carved in the shape of a skull, had a celluloid stem. Frisco rumored that the tiny bottles found by other locals could be opium bottles (or a similar type bottle used for photography chemicals). A series of "Chinese huts" remained for years in the Ten Mile to pique local curiosity, but archeologists insisted they were Italian in origin, not Chinese. Nevertheless, the connection of Orientals and electric power in Frisco remains today.

The town board granted the Frisco Light and Power Company a contract to wire the town hall and install five big 2,000-candle arc lights. Four shone on Main Street, at Second, Third, Fourth and Fifth. The last lit up Third and Galena. In a moment of political diplomacy, trustees also opted for a 50-candle light on a tree at Fifth and Galena, near the home of F. C. Dinsmore, King Solomon Mining Syndicate president.

"We are proud of the fact that our town was the first in the county to have electric arc lights in the streets," said a progressive Mayor J. Percy Hart in the *Bulletin*. "What we need next is a water and sewer system." (The mayor's statement did not prove prophetic. Frisco finally got municipal water in 1955 and sewer in the '70s.)

What the town did get was a ditch, a town water ditch, dug in 1908, that channeled water from the tumbling North Ten Mile Creek through town on Main Street. "The new ditch built for the town last summer is now running full of fresh clear water and is not only a great convenience, but also invaluable in case of fire," Mayor Hart boasted.

The ditch "ran clear" despite the questionable habits of homeowners who dumped coffee grounds, grease and refuse into the town water flow. Others dammed the ditch to create their own irrigation systems.

After a decade of achievement, the board faced 1910 with a pesky problem: "Numerous horses and cows allowed to run at large" had caused "an aggravating annoyance," launching a tirade of complaints upon the image-conscious trustees.

Unbounded optimism expanded the vision of Frisco's leaders. Embarking on a new century in 1900 had stirred hope. This fresh start, combined with a mining bonanza proved a little too much for Mayor Percy Hart to handle. In a burst of enthusiasm, he predicted in print: "It is reasonable to assume that countless millions will roll into the coffers of companies operating in the district in the next dozen years," he told July 31, 1909 *Breckenridge Bulletin* readers.

Although Frisco's mining boom would bust in the coming years,

Hart did have some good reasons for his prediction of prosperity. One factor played a vital role in realizing the hope of mining riches: Machinery magnified the workman's effort to increase output. The *Bulletin* quoted Mayor Hart:

The antiquated tools and methods employed by the prospector have been supplanted by the most improved machinery money can buy, and instead of work being carried on by a single prospector, and occasionally two of them, away upon the mountain tops, massive compressors furnish air for operating power machine drills and gangs of men are driving huge tunnels into the mountains from the lowest points to cut veins at great depths.

The improved Ingersoll power drill provides an example of a faster, expanded-scale tool that boosted efficiency. In the 1870s, miners had to "double jack," driving spikes with sledge hammers into rock to create a hole which they stuffed with blasting powder to blow out tunnels, chambers and stopes. Later dynamite, invented in time for the 1880s lode mining excitement, became the hard rock miners' boon. After 1900, steam-driven power drills like the Ingersoll reduced cave-in danger, while producing quick results. Cost in 1905 deflated dollars for Mary Verna-North American Mine drills: A sky-high $25,000.

Another reason Frisco's future looked promising lay in its capacity to attract the state's best miners by paying top wages. "Frisco is the busiest mining camp in the county," the July 31, 1909 *Bulletin* declared. Local mines paid a lavish $.31 to $.62 per hour for an eight hour work day. An average miner brought home $18.00 per six-day week or just over $70.00 per month in days when a crate of apples sold for a dime.

Frisco, forced to turn away newcomers for lack of available housing, looked to its future in 1909 and saw something akin to the Biblical Millenium. "A feeling of confidence pervades the district," the *Bulletin* glowed. After a decade of intensive, big-budget development of its mines, Frisco waited for the pure-gold payoff. The message from Frisco's crystal ball? "1909 promises to be a banner year."

A researcher who scrutinizes the Frisco area mines will observe that while countless dollars flowed into these corporate-financed ventures organized after the century's turn, very little came out. Production records are strangely absent. While 1900 newspapers proliferate with big dollar development items, news of ore shipments to smelters and annual profit reports remain slim. Removed by time

51

and undistracted by the promoter's hullabaloo, it is easy to see that Frisco's 1900-1910 mining growth became an over-inflated balloon waiting for a pin.

One mine, dazzling in its riches, bucked the trend and produced, year after year, a fortune in mineral wealth. That treasure was Mt. Royal's Victoria.

The Victoria Mine: A 1900s Profile

Located a half an hour's hike above and southwest of Frisco, the 9,600-foot high Victoria site is visible from Colorado Highway 9 at the base of a massive avalanche scar slicing the northeast face of Mt. Victoria. An avalanche once smashed the mine's early-day settlement to smithereens!

General Buford's 1866 gold-copper discovery at the Victoria grew to five lode claims and its neighboring Eureka patch boasted seven additional claims. The *Breckenridge Bulletin*, December 29, 1900, pronounced the Victoria would "undoubtedly show one of the best mines in the State."

A. E. Keables, a savvy and seasoned Breckenridge mining man, engineered an October, 1903 purchase of the prosperous Victoria and Eureka claims. New owners, the Masontown Mining and Milling Company, consolidated the claims, according to the October 1, 1903 *Mining Recorder* and promptly boosted the mine's work force from 25 to 125 men. Ore production soared and the mine's new officers built a concentrating mill, big enough to process 75 ore tons daily from the 100 acre mine.

The company's efficient mine management produced profits strong enough to enable officers to pay off its final $18,000 installment on the mine purchase.

With regular gold and silver shipments to Denver's U. S. Mint via the Colorado & Southern that served the mine, the Masontown Mining and Milling Company prepared to dismantle Breckenridge's famous Wilson smelter and move it to the Victoria site, according to an October 3, 1903 Breckenridge newspaper. Scattered bricks remain at the site today as evidence of the smelter's presence.

Frisco's 1907-08 newspaper, *The Successful Miner*, reported the 1907 transfer of the Victoria Mine from the Masontown company to the Hibbs Mining and Milling Company, noting that the new owners "offer dividend-guaranteed stock."

Mayor J. Percy Hart served as Hibbs Company secretary-treasurer in 1909. Pictured in the July 31, 1909 *Breckenridge Bulletin*, Hart appeared young and handsome, with dark hair and moustache, and a slim, athletic build. The company's big mill also appreared in a photo. A prominent 200 by 300-foot structure with a slanted tin roof visible from below, it rose against the hillside, large and imposing— and also smack in the path of the snowslide that would later cause its destruction. Hart announced in 1909 the realization of a dream held by Victoria owners for decades: To drive a tunnel from Mt. Royal's base to cut the Victoria lode at its deepest point. The new tunnel began just 90 feet above the railroad line, according to the *Bulletin*.

The King Solomon Mining Syndicate

Colonel James H. Myers, a mining promoter of titanic talent, came to Frisco in the 1890's to test his theory of "deep mining." He began in 1898 driving his King Solomon Tunnel, one-half mile south of Frisco on the Ten Mile Canyon's east wall. Meanwhile, his 1860's-founded King Solomon Mining Syndicate, propelled by Myers' steamroller zeal, managed to acquire an impressive portfolio of mines around Frisco. Myers parlayed these into an investment package that pulled unparalleled investment capital to Frisco. Almost singlehandedly, Colonel Myers, a scrawny, squint-eyed giant among men, caused mining's resurgence in the Frisco area.

The Mint

James H. "Dimp" Myers, Jr. held the superintendent's title at the Mint, one mile south of Frisco on 10,199-foot Ophir Mountain. The Mint Mining and Milling Company's 1903 prospectus said the Mint tunnel, slated for 3,000 feet, would cut seven lode claims. Dimp had built a timber house and blacksmith shop at the tunnel's mouth, the October 4, 1902 *Summit County Journal* reported. The company planned to develop a five-acre mill site in 1903. "The large property practically covers Ophir Mountain," the *Journal* said.

The *Bulletin* maintained that the Mt. Royal's famous Victoria lode crossed the Mint property, just southeast. "There is no better vein in the District."

After the hasty reorganization of the U. S. Mining Company, which formerly owned the property, Colonel Myers had renamed the Mint and quickly dispelled dark clouds of rumored fraud or embezzlement to polish the mine's image before stockholders.

The Juno

Henry Recen's early 1870s silver lode continued to operate. Its ore transport problems ceased when the railroad laid its track just

75 feet from the Juno's diggings.

The King Solomon Mine

The well-heeled King Solomon Mining Syndicate penetrated Mt. Royal's west slope in the Ten Mile Canyon. By working three shifts to push the tunnel day and night, the King Solomon bore aimed to reach 12 to 17 "very strong" lodes. The mine's steep payroll, $3,500 monthly, reflected its use of triple shifts. Myers first planned the tunnel for 3,000 feet, but cash from eager investors from New York, Cleveland, Chicago, St. Louis, and places in Pennsylvania and Wisconsin financed further excavation. Dimp Myers took over as King Solomon Mine superintendent around 1905 and strove for 100-foot monthly progress. By 1909, the *Breckenridge Bulletin* noted an impressive 3,000-foot progress on the eight by eight foot tunnel, which moved ahead by 10 feet every 24 hours. Newspapers reported pockets of "pure metallic gold" enroute, along with stunning shot and wire gold nuggets.

The 1909 article detailed the 600-acre mine's modern equipment, including a powerful 163-horsepower Heine water tube boiler for steam production and a mammoth Ingersoll-Sargent air compressor, specially designed for high altitude, that could power eight of the large 3 ¼ inch drills or 15 to 20 small drills. The C&S ran past the power plant. The mine had a six-car rail spur to the tunnel with a chute to dump ore directly into rail cars.

Five years after the *Bulletin* report, Dillon's *Blue Valley Times* announced, "The King Solomon will resume work in its 7,000-foot tunnel." Local excavator, Wayne Bristol, contracted to re-open the King Solomon in recent years. Bristol found the solid rock tunnel in perfect shape. "A beauty," he said. No cave-in has occurred because the tunnel is solid rock.

The Mary Verna

Locals remember the big power house beside the rail track at the Ten Mile Canyon's Mary Verna, about 1 ½ miles from Frisco. Its gray and brown tailings dump serves as a landmark today. H. T. McAlister, a big, heavy-set graying man, held the mine manager's post at the Mary Verna in 1909. The mine's 1,621-foot tunnel into Peak One's solid granite face required use of Leyner water-air drills and a Leyner air compressor. "An electric generator furnishes incandescent light for both mines [the Mary Verna and its neighbor, the North American], and all buildings," the *Bulletin* reported.

In 1909, the mine consolidated with the North American and had

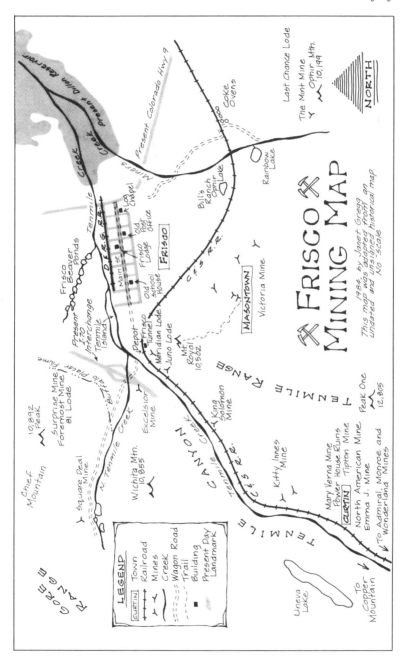

already bought out a large number of claims known as The Old Guard Group, to become the largest mine in the district.

The North American

Pushing its tunnel to 2,557 feet, the North American boasted a first class 20-horsepower exhaust fan that kept its air unpolluted. "Within 20 minutes of firing a round of shots (blasting), every particle of smoke and foul air has been removed from the tunnel," the July 31, 1909 *Breckenridge Bulletin* said.

These fine gadgets were paraded before visiting dignitaries. "J. H. Myers, Jr. of Frisco entertained a party of Eastern excursionists yesterday," a 1903 *Summit County Journal* article said. They are on a tour of inspection of the mineral resources in the Frisco district," Among a group touring the North American and Mary Verna was E. C. Gilliland of Memphis, Tennessee.

The Kitty Innes

Henry Learned's silver lode, the Kitty Innes, continued from its 1879 discovery until the 1893 Silver Panic. In the 1900 mining surge, the Kitty Innes received a flurry of mentions in the *Breckenridge Bulletin*. Located on the rail line, the mine stood in an advantageous ore shipping spot. Whether the Kitty Innes participated in the Canyon's deep tunnel gold mining boom remains uncertain. In 1909, after Learned's death, the mine stood idle as negotiations on its purchase continued.

The Admiral

The Admiral planned in 1900 to drive its tunnel until "old Judson Mountain is cut through," the December 29, *Bulletin* announced. The effort received a *Montezuma Prospector* mention in 1906: "The Admiral Tunnel will push another 1,000 feet into the Ten Mile Range this summer." Involved in stockholder dispute, the Admiral, located four miles south of Frisco in the Canyon, shut down in 1909.

The Monroe

Owned by Warren and Belford in 1897, the Monroe produced gold ore with a high iron sulphide content and a smidgen of copper. Chauncey Carlisle Warren worked the property in 1901, according to the February 20, 1901 *Denver Times*. The Monroe had followed a vein 290 feet and hit a six-foot-wide ore streak. Warren, the *Times* said, "got a carload of machinery and is to build a tramway from the mine to the railroad." Warren's tramway and wooden tower, plus a lone cabin perched high in the gulch, marked the Monroe Mine for sightseers and joyriding teenagers for many decades to follow.

Chief Mountain Mines

The Chief Mining and Milling Company, successor to the old Foremost property, perched at the very pinnacle of 11,363-foot Chief Mountain. Known as "the mountain of lead," Chief yielded ore running 90 percent lead, practically solid galena, according to the 1909 *Bulletin*. Early day prospectors here struggled along a precarious trail to transport ore via burro pack trains before they abandoned the Foremost claim. Modern machinery resurrected the Foremost and Surprise claims here. In 1909 the *Bulletin* declared, "The Foremost is the only real lead mine in the whole district as gold predominates in all the others." A few years later, the *Blue Valley Times* reported, "The Chief Mountain Mining Company shipped $10,000 worth of lead sulphide from the Surprise vein."

Buffalo Placers

The rotting water flume clinging to Chief Mountain's rocky flank (visible from the Frisco I-70 exit 201 east bound on-ramp) represents a futile effort by the Buffalo Placers Company to transport North Ten Mile Creek water to Salt Lick Gulch (near today's Wildernest). The enterprising Colonel Lemuel Kingsberry managed a hydraulic mining operation there that gained prominence after 1900. Ranchers holding prior water rights squashed the Colonel's visionary water transfer plans.

The Square Deal

At the west Frisco I-70 interchange is the North Ten Mile Creek's mouth. About one mile in on this creek was the Square Deal Mine. Capitalized at $2 million, the Square Deal Company planned a 162-acre townsite near Frisco, three major tunnels to penetrate Chief Mountain and predicted "ore enough to last centuries." The mine, situated on one of old J. D. Hynderliter's ranches, displayed much promotional activity, but little production. Colonel Myers, by 1906 living in Montezuma as editor of the *Montezuma Prospector*, nicknamed it the "Crooked Deal Mine."

Myers embellished his "crooked deal" slur with a printed accusation that Square Deal president Frank E. Wire promoted and sold fraudulent stock. "Show me one bill of lading for an ore shipment," Myers screamed. (Colonel Myers' own personal integrity failed to shine under the limelight's glare.) The squealing Mr. Wire responded with a scalding letter which the *Breckenridge Bulletin* headlined, "Frank E. Wire Goes After Myers' Scalp." "Myers exaggerates and has been involved in some shady deals in Cleveland," Wire charged. Few could get the last word with Colonel Myers. He had a newspaper as his soapbox, a scalpel-sharp editor's pen, and a wit to match.

The Square Deal escaped with the shreds of its reputation and continued to drive its main tunnel reaching 2,090 feet in July, 1909 and pushing past 2,300 feet later. Ed Huter, who also ran a miners' boarding house in Frisco, managed the mine as superintendent in 1909. The Square Deal, with mine office, barn, three tunnels and a mill plus cabins, bustled into 1910. A good wagon road connected the mill with the railroad at the narrow North Ten Mile Canyon's mouth.

The Excelsior

As travelers approach the Ten Mile Canyon, 10,855-foot Wichita Peak stands as a sentinel guarding the canyon's entrance on the west, across from a twin watchtower, Mt. Royal. Just inside the canyon, in a cleft on Wichita's slope, is the Excelsior Mine, locally famed as the first in the district to produce and use electricity. The power operated a large concentrating mill, processing ore from the Excelsior's tunnel and a later shaft. Mill structure remains are clearly visible beside the old Excelsior dump here. The concentrating mill, with its massive timbers now crumbling, went up in 1898, when Dan Recen's old mine re-opened under Wyborg & Ault. Fifteen men worked through the winter in 1901, according to the April 18, 1901 *Bulletin*. In 1903, the mine busily produced copper and lead. The Excelsior shipped three carloads of ore in 1906 that showed its mineral content—20 ounces silver per ton, two and one-half ounces gold and 30 percent lead.

In 1909, Edward Bonnell, a tall, lanky, bald man with a penetrating gaze, managed the Excelsior. The mine had a railroad spur that began south of the mill and climbed the hill, passing the mine office building. This building later became the Allen family's Frisco home.

Railroads and Real Estate

The reader might assume that the shrewd Colonel James H. Myers, who had his facile hand in most of Frisco's important mines, would be too busy to meddle in the affairs of, say, the Colorado & Southern Railroad.

Not so.

Consider the case of the town's railroad lots, a suspicious deal that one Frisco official called "a palpable fraud." In, 1901, Elijah K. Bailey, posing as a trustee of the Colorado & Southern Railroad, secured from the Frisco town board deeds to all forfeited town lots given to the rail company under the town's 1883 agreement. The C&S had never accepted the deeds in the 1880s, having little interest in the Frisco town fathers' gift. Then Bailey, who was Colonel Myers' brother-in-law recently transplanted from Iowa, joined Myers in a visit to the C&S railroad executive offices. There the visitors offered to split the land. To the sellers' dismay, the railroad officials turned the pair down flat—several times—and wrote a scalding letter to the Frisco town board describing the double-dealing affair.

The outraged town board wrote Elijah K. Bailey a registered letter demanding he return the deeds to the lots. When the reprobate Bailey did so, the C&S issued a quit claim deed to the town of Frisco, for $1 consideration, transferring "all rights, title, interest and demand" to the deeds, except blocks 31-35 and 42-48.

Ten Mile Canyon's Curtin station served Mary Verna, North American mines.
Recen Family Photo

Then the mud slinging began. Colonel Myers integrity came into question over the unscrupulous town lot deal. A Breckenridge newspaper published a letter from a Frisco town official charging Myers with mine fraud at the Mint, financial "irregularities" as Frisco town clerk and trickery over the town lots. Myers' retort, laced with verbal peppercorns, made headlines the next week. The Frisco official countered, "The rock must have hit Myers for he's the only one squealing."

Colonel Myers remained unscathed by the front-page slug-out. He philosophized:

> The man that lacks energy to excite a protest—the devil does not want him and in Heaven there is no room for him. The great achievements of this world have been accomplished against the protest of the multitude.

Colonel Myers reminded readers that General Ulysses S. Grant and General Robert E. Lee had also received severe criticism.

Historic Log Schoolhouse

Frisco school board president John D. Hynderliter felt the pressure in 1900 to keep his eyes open for property to erect a new schoolhouse. Frisco experienced a flood of newcomers, so many that residential housing for the horde ran out. As class sizes increased, school district secretary Frank Cherryholmes recorded the board's growing disenchantment with the 1899 school.

Early records of Frisco's Summit School District No. 9 still remain in the Colorado State Archives. Their yellowed pages, peppered with poor grammar and misspelled words, document the purchase of the log school building, which still stands today on Frisco's Main Street. The log structure, in use till 1980 as county schools administration building, boasts a wonderful Victorian belltower, taken from Breckenridge's 1882 four-room school, a gem designed by Victorian architect, Elias Nashold.

Voters passed the bond election to fund the schoolhouse on October 5, 1901. On November 22, 1901, the school board decided not to build, but to buy an existing building, the Schloss building on Second and Main. The price tag: $1,500, paid November 30, 1901.

Mildly shocking was the fact that the prim schoolhouse had been constructed as a saloon by 46-year old miner, Oliver Swanson. The 1889 Swedish immigrant bought his land from the town on April 18, 1900 for $25. Teacher Minnie Campbell and 1900 school term students watched the log building progress from the windows of their existing schoolhouse just across Second Avenue on Main

Street. On May 5, 1900, the *Breckenridge Bulletin* reported that Mr. Swanson's 25 by 52-foot "new building is gradually growing." Kids who should have been studying geography stared fascinated as Henry Recen, Sr. hewed the exterior logs smooth. A bricklayer later appeared to build a fine chimney and a worker laid a rock-lined wine cellar in the cool basement. (Children would be surprised next fall to see the saloon's oak back bar, mirror, oak ice chest and oak cigar case moved out and their school desks moved in for the 1902 term. A curious switch: The site of the children's old school is today itself a "saloon," the Moose Jaw.)

In 1901, the new saloon went out of business. The building sold to Simon Schloss, Lake City, Colorado on October 9, 1901. On November 30, the building came into the hands of Frisco School District No. 9 for a cost of $1,500.

Soon after the sale took place, Miss Lula Orsburn waltzed onto the Frisco scene. Sweet Lula, a demure and modest young lady, would cause a ruckus with Frisco's three hard-boiled school board members that created newspaper headlines, a court battle and caught the young miss a husband—none other than Colonel Myers' jovial son, Dimp.

Like many young country girls who finished school in those days, Lula Orsburn studied to pass the exam for a teacher's certificate.

When she heard that the 1901-term Frisco teacher had vacated her post, Lula landed the job. (The outgoing schoolmarm, Charlotte McDonald of Kokomo, was the sister of Elizabeth McDonald Giberson, mother of the Giberson family that lived and ranched near Frisco over many decades.)

The 1902-03 Frisco Teacher's Daily register shows, in Lula's own hand, her class list of 26 students.

Her list reads:

Name	Grade	Age
Allen, Francis	4th	10
Allen, Ora	1st	6
Britton, Willis	3rd	7
Brown, Grace	5th	11
Brown, Tom	7th	14
Brown, Cora	3rd	8
Colcord, Rex	6th	—
Brown, Eugene	2nd	7
Harper, Mable	1st	10
Harper, Willie	3rd	12

Harper, Frank	1st	6
Harper, Myrtle	5th	14
Harper, Pearl	5th	16
Linquist, Marie	3rd	8
Linquist, Annie	5th	12
Markey, Margaret	3rd	12
Markey, James	2nd	7
Markey, Michael	1st	5
Smith, Edna	5th	12
Staley, Addie	4th	11
Staley, Ben	4th	14
Staley, Elva(Edna?)	1st	6
Thomas, Nellie	3rd	9
Wood, Agnes	6th	13
Busby, Geraldine	3rd	8
Linquist, Edith	7th	14

Lula coped with the problems of her class—such as a 10-year old in grade one—with her own special qualities: Sympathy, a listening ear and a love for children.

Despite these traits remembered by her friends, and not-with-standing her quiet and gentle nature, Miss Lula Lillian Orsburn stirred up the biggest fuss the Frisco school board had ever seen!

School board meeting records sail along serenely, with no hint of trouble, until December 24, 1902, when the three- man school board called a special Christmas Eve meeting to discuss their young teacher's contract. The minutes, with all their misspellings, read:

> Resolved that the contract heretofore existing between the School Board of District No 9 of Frisco Summit co, Colo and Miss Lula Orsburn be and the Same hereby is Terminated for the reason that the Servises rendered by the said Miss Lula Orsburn air unsatisfactory and not in accordance with the terms of said contract... Motion made and carried that the warrant Due Mis Orsburn for the month of December should not be given to her untill she render a term report. and Deliver the Key which is now in her posession unto the board

The reason for the Christmas Eve purge may remain a mystery. The plain facts are that Lula Orsburn was fired, her contract revoked and her salary withheld. What was the schoolmarm's side of the story? An amusing explanation was offered more than 75 years later by one of Lula's students, Frisco-born Marie Linquist, who became Marie Linquist Marshall Rennick. Mrs. Rennick told her story to

Summit Historical Society curator Naomi Fleming, who recorded these notes:

> There were "three old bachelors" on the Frisco school board, two in love with Lula. They resented Dimp's courtship of Lula, as miners were not well regarded in Frisco. When Lula returned to Frisco... these bachelors had nailed boards across the doors of the school to bar her... The parents resolved the situation, and at the end of the year, Lula married Dimp.

Stinging from the injury to her reputation, the loss of her position and the broken contract, plucky Lula Orsburn filed suit against Summit School District No. 9, Frisco, on February 11, 1903.

She sued for compensation for her suspension as a contract teacher. In choosing to file a county court suit, young Lula went to war with three powerful local residents, John D. Hynderliter, H. E. Heckman and William Vanatta, the school board president, treasurer and secretary, respectively.

Hynderliter, called a "pioneer Frisco miner" by *The Successful Miner*, a short-lived 1907 Frisco newspaper, worked his General Meade Mine atop Mt. Royal for many years, determined to reach the gold he knew lay locked within—but he never made the big strike. He was an old man who "boasted a strong physique. He climbs mountains regularly and packs 50 pounds of groceries to his summer cabin," *The Successful Miner* reported. Hynderliter, with an unkempt black moustache and beard, had a sinister facial expression enhanced by dry, deeply wrinkled leathery skin and bony, beak nose. His appearance hints that Hynderliter was capable of scaring timid young teachers during six years-plus as a school board member. He was a hard man to stand up to.

Sixty-seven year old John D. Hynderliter, a widower for many years, had come to the Rocky Mountains at age 45. On August 20, 1887, he took up a 160-acre ranch in the North Ten Mile, which he later sold to the Square Deal Mining Company, finally making his lucky strike—in real estate! Later, he owned a second ranch in east Frisco. Finally as a dying man, he sold his General Meade to Percy Hart's Frisco Mining, Milling and Development Company.

Hynderliter himself assumed responsibility for squashing Lula's legal suit. He also hired a lawyer to represent the school board—none other than the county school superintendent's new husband, attorney J. T. Hogan!

Hogan, a well-known Breckenridge lawyer had married Lulu Buffington in a Christmas, 1902 ceremony. The new Mrs. Hogan faced an unusual conflict of interest.

Meanwhile James H. Myers, Jr., managing the Mint Mine on Ophir Mountain at the time, courted the disconcerted Miss Orsburn. A serious relationship had blossomed. On June 20, the *Breckenridge Bulletin* had the pleasure of announcing the pair's surprise wedding at the Orsburn ranch near Elizabeth, Colorado.

Dimp Myers broke up the board's trio of crabby bachelors by running—and winning—in the May, 1905 school district elections. Soon Lula's sister, Miss Lucy Orsburn stepped in as teacher for two terms beginning September 5, 1905 and ending in May, 1907. The board loosened its formerly tight grip on the purse strings to allow Lucy Orsburn to buy "curtains and such school supplies as necessary" and to provide cash for railroad "fair" to travel to a Denver teachers' convention.

The board appointed 31-year old Marguerite Detwiler both teacher and Frisco school principal in 1908. Another Detwiler, this time Florence, taught Frisco students in 1910.

Despite school board squabbles and primitive conditions, such as the old woodstove that roasted pupils nearby and failed to warm those a ways off, Frisco children had fun. Children hunted spring blossoms and birds in a May 5, 1900 outing reported by the *Breckenridge Bulletin*:

> The school of this place has closed a pleasant year of 8 months. A visit to the woods, under the auspices of the Bird Club constituted a pleasing feature to the closing exercises.

Frisco's early day students remember countless trips to the water cooler in the corner with its generous long handled dipper. (They were probably followed by countless trips to the two outhouses in the schoolyard.) One student, Anne Giberson Dale, recalled the glaring gaze of President Washington's portrait, his eyes following her to the cooler and back. (The nostalgic dipper may have contributed to the wildfire spread of epidemics in Summit's early day schools, such as the October, 1907 scarlet fever epidemic.) Frisco's scarred old-fashioned desks, displayed today in the Summit Historical Society museum in Dillon, bear lofty inscriptions, such as "Strive and Win," "Improve the Times," "Aim High," "Patience Wins," and "Be Kind" and "Be True."

Local poet Lillian MacMasters expressed Frisco schoolchildren's remembered fondness for "The Little Log Schoolhouse":

> Yes! I'm dreaming tonight of a schoolhouse of logs

Nestling deep in the Rockies - out West -
And I'd rather be there, with my youth, and old togs
Than be President Roosevelt's guest.

Frisco's Women: "As WE Say"

Local gentlemen lifted eyebrows over the passage of women's
suffrage in Colorado in 1900. Frisco women had organized an election day strike, but called it off and turned out in full force for the
November, 1900 presidential elections. The *Breckenridge Bulletin*,
November 10, 1900, asserted that the ladies came to do honor to
their suffrage, not for candy and "as WE say."

While the ladies received a new freedom, Frisco's male drinking
set had theirs curtailed. Mayor Percy Hart hired a police judge to
assist the town marshall and declared: "The saloons must be run
as any other business would be and drunkeness and fighting will
not be tolerated." The new police judge added muscle to His Honor's
desire to "impress upon the minds of wrong-doers that law and
order must prevail."

An unofficial assistant to the police justice was tiny Mrs. Jane
Thomas, a diminutive but determined lady who helped keep the
peace on Main Street. Between the Thomas and Linquist hotels sat
a saloon that often erupted in drunken brawls. According to a Linquist family member, Marie Linquist Rennick, a fight broke out in
the saloon one night. ("There were saloons everywhere," she remembered.) Bystanders attempted to stop the fray, but failed. The
fight became nasty. A knife appeared and one man took several
serious slashes. Then the tenacious Mrs. Thomas, a woman never
tall enough to look the assailant in the eye, intervened. Her secret
strength: The force of her gentle and persuasive personality, according to Mrs. Rennick.

Working wives, a much-discussed phenomenon in today's society, are really nothing new. "My mother ran the [Frisco] Hotel and
my Dad worked in the mines," remembered Ida Linquist Murphy
in a 1984 letter about her Frisco childhood days. Frisco women ran
hotels, boarding houses and general stores. They cooked for hungry
workers at area mines and taught school. They also found time to
nurse the sick, mother local orphans, milk cows, bake bread and
attend births as midwives.

Women also served as volunteers. When Colonel James H. Myers'
daughter, Mattie, wasn't working as a public relations girl escorting
visiting investors to Syndicate-managed mines, she did "church

work." According to Marie Linquist Rennick, Mattie Myers dressed up as a nun and went about Frisco soliciting donations for the Catholic Church.

Frisco never got a church in the early days, despite Mattie Myers' effort. When itinerant preachers held services in Main Street hotels, the sound of hymns would pour into an unsanctified Main Street, more used to dance hall cacophony. Hotels became the scene of weddings, too, such as the Christmas Eve, 1902 marriage of Miss Nellie Rose to Mr. John Deming, at the Thomas Hotel. "Not less than 50 persons" witnessed the ceremony, which "took place between two well filled and illuminated Christmas trees, under a canopy of evergreen and orange blossoms," according to the family's yellowed newspaper clippings. The Deming family remained in Frisco for over 60 years.

"Thoroughly modern" Frisco boasted not only electric lights, "running water" (the new town ditch) and telephone service in the early 1900s. A prominent businessman, hotel owner C. O. Linquist, drove an automobile down Main Street one memorable day in 1904. "My Dad brought the first car to Frisco in 1904—a Stanley Steamer. What excitement!" wrote Ida Linquist Murphy. "I don't recall that it was too successful, however," she added.

A newspaper, *The Successful Miner*, first rolled off ink-stained iron presses in 1907. The weekly shone among its competitors as a model of fair, objective reporting. While *Summit County Journal* editor Fincher labeled his rival paper, "the Dillon Crossing Foghorn" and *Montezuma Prospector* editor Colonel James H. Myers blatantly used his position to advance his own mining properties, Frisco's *Successful Miner* published informative reports devoid of invective or slander. Small wonder, then, that it lasted only two years, meeting its demise in 1909.

Frisco's gaiety and optimism in the early 1900s mirrored that of the lusty 1880s, when the town's mushrooming growth burst forth with new faces, new buildings, a parade of colorful events. For the man who watched the pendulum swing from high point to high point, an era ended. The man who named the yet unbirthed town in 1875 and helped found the community in 1879, who served as mayor, trustee, recorder, postmaster and Kitty Innes Mine discoverer, Henry Learned, died in 1903 at age 83.

CHAPTER 5

A Town Becomes a Community

You'll find a whittling-piece today
Up by the depot where he waited
Timeless at the canyon mouth
Whittling, pondering away.
He had a joke. He used to say
'Guess we lost her, guess she's gone
Up the wrong canyon.' Hours belated
His ancient arms received the mail,
His ancient legs began to wamble
After his handcart down the trail.
You'll find a whittling-piece today
And all your fiery impotence,
All the blisters of delay
Will cool away, will cool away.
  (Belle Turnbull, *The Tenmile Range*)

Frisco's Lifeline: The Narrow Gauge

Twin arteries, pulsating lifeblood to the heart of Frisco, were the two railroads that served the town. The tough little steam locomotives, spraying cinders and puffing smoke, chugged into town each day, bringing beans, bacon and tea, laced-trimmed camisoles and top hats, U. S. mail and mining tools. Both the C&S (nicknamed "Crooked & Slow") and the D&RG ("The Little Giant") labored and lurched their way through the mine-riddled Ten Mile Canyon, stopping at over a dozen loading stations to pick up the district's gold, silver lead and zinc ores.

Before World War I broke out in Europe, both mountain railways came to a screeching, deadening halt. Colorado & Southern Railway officials in 1911 cut service to Summit County, complaining that the company lost a million dollars annually on the branch from Como over Boreas Pass to Breckenridge. The C&S continued to Dickey (today's Farmers Korner) where the rails split, one branch serving

Dillon and Keystone; the other branch swinging west to Frisco, the Ten Mile and Fremont Pass. The C&S' colorful "High Line," the nation's highest railway, served America's highest postoffice atop Boreas Pass, the only U. S. postal station to straddle the Continental Divide. The railroad company's main gripe focused on this 21-mile Boreas Pass section of track, which officials insisted would cost $325,000 to properly maintain. The *Blue Valley Times* retorted that $325,000 was peanuts to a company that had just paid its stockholders a whopping $13 million in 1911 dividends. And the Railroad Commission ran screaming into court with an expert witness' estimate of $100 to rejuvenate the Boreas track.

The C&S had refused to honor the Railroad Commission's 1911 ruling that ordered the railway to "reinstate daily through passenger trains each way and freight service each way three times per week over the South Park Line on or after January 1, 1912." C&S officials maintained that the commission had no authority to dictate their financial decisions. Leadville District Court Judge Cavendar overruled the C&S, declaring the Railroad Commission a legal body, according to an April 26, 1912 *Blue Valley Times* report. The C&S steamrolled the case into the U. S. Supreme Court. On January 23, 1913 the Supreme Court upheld the Railroad Commission on every point and reaffirmed the validity of a steep $1,000 per day fine imposed over a year earlier by the Colorado Supreme Court on January 1, 1912.

On January 24, 1913, a rankled C&S Railway resumed service over Boreas Pass to Summit County. "Trains Again Move" exulted a *Blue Valley Times* January 24 headline. The company took its financial lumps and maintained continual (and continually late) service to Summit County until 1937.

The shutdown, lasting more than a year, followed by a hike in freight and passenger fares in Summit County only, squeezed Frisco's mine-centered economy.

The district doubled over from a second blow when the Denver & Rio Grande discontinued its Blue River branch in 1912. The 8 a.m. train from Leadville had screeched into Frisco every day before lunch and continued to Dillon, arriving there at 12:13 p.m. The train returned, passing again through Frisco just north of Main Street and steaming into the Canyon to arrive in Leadville before sunset.

But no more. Before anyone began a protest, the D&RG tore up its track, dismantled its trestles, relocated its big 47,500 gallon water tanks and disappeared from the Ten Mile Canyon, closing the door on its 30-year railroading history there.

No rail service at all in 1912 created a dismal situation for a district producing low grade ore, dependent on efficient low-cost freight transportation to make mining profits.

No "All Aboard"

No shrill whistle floated on the air, no squealing racket of swaying cars, no heartbeat chuga-chuga-chug echoed off canyon walls. Frisco sat in grim silence and watched its mining life slowly die. Even with resumption of C&S service at increased rates in 1913, Frisco's mining never recovered.

Trends in metal prices ganged up to finish off Frisco's mining demise. The district's galena-rich ores contained a high zinc and lead content. The old-timers had discarded zinc in their mill dumps, but after 1900, smelting techniques emerged to effectively separate silver and zinc. Summit County produced 13 million pounds of zinc, ranking third in the state, according to the U. S. Geological Survey's Charles Henderson. But zinc prices plummeted in 1912, leaving Frisco mine owners empty-handed. Lead also took a downhill slide from 1905 to 1922, Henderson pointed out. By 1918, World War I's final year, Colorado had experienced a sickening crunch in metal production. Combined metals prices had dropped 19 percent, Henderson's *Mining In Colorado* stated. Even the Climax Molybdenum Mill shut down in April, 1919.

Frisco's mines never ground to a halt; they just slowed their breakneck pace and began to plod. The Excelsior, under Captain J. A. Hassel's management, shipped four or five railroad cars of ore to the smelter each month in 1912. The never-say-die King Solomon Mining Syndicate drove its King Solomon tunnel to 7,000 feet by January, 1913, according to Dillon's *Blue Valley Times*. The Square Deal Company folded and Ed Huter, hired as superintendent, grabbed the property when it went up for bid in March, 1913.

In February, 1913, the Frisco Light & Power Company flicked off the lights in Frisco and closed its doors, leaving the *Blue Valley Times* to bemoan the loss in a February 19 article. The town came close to losing telephone service as well in January, 1913. Fire destroyed Prestrud's store and, with it, the telephone exchange. The volunteer fire department hacked in vain at a frozen town water ditch.

Firefighters fought frigid temperatures and frozen water supplies as well as deep drifts, for in 1913 relentless snows piled up record accumulations, according to the late Helen Rich's *Empire* magazine article, "The Years It Snowed." Prestrud's store may have run low on supplies before it burned, because a railroad blockade occurred that winter, Rich wrote.

Going back to 1913: There was another memorable blockade. That was the time the whisky supply ran short—food, too—but the whisky shortage caused the greater alarm. The saloonkeepers rose to that crisis, however. They replenished the kegs with potato parings, pepper and water, along with other ingredients they considered relevant. The brew was pure fire and gall, but it was potent and customers were not lacking. When the first train rolled into camp that spring (those were the days of the narrow-gauge, abandoned in 1938), the whole camp turned out to help unload. What was the first item to be handed down amid rousing cheers? That's right.

The Old Postoffice

Despite the dirth of a warming nip of brandy for encouragement, Friscoans restored telephone service, this time in Louis A. Wildhack's home, which he converted to a store.

Helen Foote, owner of Louis Wildhack's historic home, wrote in a recent application to the National Registry of Historic Landmarks:

In the late 1800's, the post office and general store was the place where everyone met. The citizens, miners, and loggers

Colorado & Southern rail cars litter curve, highlighting frequent disasters in alpine railroading.   *Recen Family Photo*

discussed politics, school problems, births, deaths, as they waited for the mail to arrive...

Louis A. Wildhack, a miner and engineer, began the construction of the building in the late 1800's. His one-room cabin eventually grew in size as he "added on" room after room as his needs required. That original room became the store and postoffice in 1914 when Wildhack became the fifth postmaster for the Town of Frisco. From this room he conducted his duties until the early 1930's.

Wildhack, a Frisco resident since the 1880s and mining surveyor during the mining boom days, received his appointment as postmaster on December 11, 1914. He served a record (and exact to the day) 21 years on the job, until December 11, 1935. His home at 510 Main Street continued to house the postoffice, under new ownership, until 1966, more than half a century.

Wildhack's one-room cabin grew as the store-postoffice became established. The postoffice and store, cramped into a tiny space in what is today part of Mrs. Foote's living room, offered only a place to pick up mail and a few supplies, such as horehound drops from the glassed candy showcase under the front counter, or tinned fruit from the wall shelves. Extra stock was shelved behind a curtain. A gilded cash register rested on the counter. The postoffice, with its ornate brass boxes and wood-slatted window, occupied the east side of the room and Wildhack's mining engineer "office" took a corner. "It was crowded when people came in to get mail off the afternoon train. If eight or 10 people were standing around and the train was late, it got very crowded," William A. Wildhack, the postmaster's son, remembered.

The 1920s addition, an extension to the east, used lumber from the Ten Mile Canyon's Admiral Mine. After the Admiral shut down around 1910, the younger Wildhack explained, Louis Wildhack made the owners a deal: If Wildhack could have the buildings as "commission," he would arrange to sell the mine's machinery at the best possible prices. Wildhack got his deal and the Admiral's sturdy structures, including the power plant building, boarding-house and tunnel portal building. The two Wildhacks, father and son, dismantled the mine structures and hauled the huge beams and planks four miles down the Canyon to their Frisco home. Some old miners, prospectors that the elder Wildhack had grubstaked, helped excavate for the new store-postoffice addition and the Admiral Mine lumber built the new room, plus others in the crazy-quilt house. Young William built a three-story chimney from the addition's basement using handmade concrete blocks. A new, roomier postoffice ran along the right wall as customers entered and a spacious store occupied the addition's left half.

Mail arrived at the Frisco depot at the town's west end. "The depot was a small building which looked more like a tool shed. It "was back toward the mountains surrounded by evergreen trees," wrote J. J. Gotch in a 1968 letter. "Mail was delivered from the train to the P.O. via sled and dogs." In summer, postmaster Wildhack used a handcart.

During Frisco's sleepy years, the postoffice emerged as the town's social hub, a place for meeting and exchanging news and gossip. "Our recreation was going to the postoffice to pick up the mail and get a few groceries," Faye Turner Korthius recalled. The old postoffice remains preserved at 510 Main Street, a fond memory for Frisco old-timers.

Sunbonnets in the Board Room

During the dismal early teen years, when Frisco lost electricity, the railroads quit and mining deflated like a balloon losing air, Frisco's town board floundered. Town meetings lapsed in May, 1913 due to lack of a quorum and no trustees met for almost three years. Then things changed— but good!

Frisco's indignant female citizens refused to sit still for the trustees' sluggard behavior any longer. They organized a town election and put their names on the ballot. "Frisco Women Seize Town Board," an April 8, 1916 *Summit County Journal* announced in shocked headline type. "Will run town affairs... propose to wipe out debt..." a dazed *Journal* report continued.

The ladies had rushed to Frisco's rescue. The lily white hand holding the gavel was new mayor Florence Huter. Trustees were Anna Mallory (she was the town midwife), Otillia "Tilly" Olson, Rena Rouse, Lizzie Tubbs, Lizzie Wildhack and Etta Wiley. Token man on the board: Louis A. Wildhack, town clerk.

A volley of small fists hammered the table as the ladies called for fiscal responsibility. They agreed to serve without pay and extended this noble gesture to clerk Wildhack as well. They slapped former town treasurer, Peter Prestrud, with a bill for eight percent interest on town funds of $139.80 held in trust by him. The ladies attacked the town's bills and vowed to make Frisco debt-free.

In 1917, the popular Mrs. Con Ecklund took the mayor's job and the town board remained primarily female. Though Frisco's menfolk returned to the town board (Louis Wildhack served as 1919 mayor), the ladies had saved the day and continued their tradition of service as trustees.

Ranch Life

The broad "park" that 1870s journalists mentioned in writing about Frisco lies partially submerged by Dillon Reservoir waters today. The flat mountain-rimmed basin, grassy and watered by clear streams and rivers, provided a perfect setting for high country ranching.

Wilbert "Wib" and Elizabeth Ann "Mollie" Giberson, newlyweds in 1904, dreamed of homesteading a ranch near Frisco. The pair honeymooned at the Ten Mile Canyon's Uneva Lake, soon moved to nearby Curtin, where their first son, Jim, was born, then lived at the Excelsior Mine camp. Later the Gibersons again crossed the Canyon, where Wib worked two jobs, one at the North American Mine and a second shift logging—long hours in days when men worked hard, but Wib was saving for his dream. After a time living in Frisco, where Wib again labored like a dynamo, the Gibersons bought a ranch two miles east of town. They planted hay and harvested in August after their second son, Roy, was born. Wib slashed with a scythe and Mollie raked the hay into huge piles to load in the wagon for delivery to the barn. There little Jim watched a third boy child, the newborn Howard, tucked carefully in the hay.

Wilbert homesteaded an adjoining 160 acres, fulfilling the requirement to live on the land, farm a section of it and prove this to the U. S. Land Office before receiving a land grant. Giberson's bore President Woodrow Wilson's signature.

The family, multiplying with Glenn, Kenneth and Edith Mary "Sue", outgrew its two-room cabin home. Wib added four rooms and later dug a well so that Mollie need no longer haul endless bucket loads of wash water to boil on the woodstove to wash clothes for seven. The ranch produced rich cream, butter and milk, eggs and poultry to add to the breads, pies and cakes that came steaming from Mollie's oven. As the Giberson children grew, friends joined them at the big ranch table. People were always welcome. Card parties at the ranch included Bill and Minnie Dusing Thomas, Lula and Dimp Myers, always with families included (no babysitters then) and laughter filled the house. As years passed, early day dances highlight many Friscoans memories. Here, Lura Belle Giberson writes about Mollie's love of fun in *Women As Tall As Our Mountains*, a wonderful series of profiles published by the local P.E.O.

FRISCO!

Chapter:

Company and dances were the main entertainment in those days. A dance in Frisco was a big event. Mollie would see that each one had his turn in the old wash tub in front of the wood heater in the living room if it was Saturday night. She would heat rocks in the oven and loaded with rocks, blankets and a fur lap robe, the entire family would pile in the sleigh and go to the dance. The children would play until they were tired, then Mollie would make beds on the chairs in the dance hall where they would sleep while the grown-ups danced. If no dance had been pre-arranged, several would go over to Ike Rouse's maybe late in the evening and throw rocks at his upstairs window and tell him that they wanted to dance. He would dress and come over to the hall.

While Ike played the fiddle, Ben Staley or Ike's wife, Mary, would chord on the piano. Sometimes Ben called for the dancers' favorite, a quadrille.

Mary Ruth, born in Breckenridge in 1902, lived on dairy ranches at today's Farmers Korner and on the Lower Blue. She rode with family and friends to the gay Frisco dances in a hay wagon. "We dolled up fit to kill," she recalled. "Mama made my clothes... we wouldn't think of going to a dance not dressed up."

The Giberson's niece, daughter of Lige and Carrie Giberson, grew up on a Frisco area ranch. Ann Giberson Dale's memories of ranch life 1910-1920 send a feeling of the warmth and richness she enjoyed:

Happy memories of the ranch include skiing and sledding down the hill behind the house; watching for the blue May flowers first appearance as the snow melted in the spring and gathering the columbines on the hillside... On the ranch I also remember the "ice house" where large chunks of ice were stored with sawdust. The ice was sawed and stored in the winter for use in the summer months such as for making ice cream on the Fourth of July and for other purposes. There was a "meat house" also where meat was hung and Dad would cut it as needed on the butcher block. Summit county weather provided the refrigeration. There was also a "milk house" where the cream separator was located and water from a deep well was used in a water cooling system to cool the milk stored there, some of which was sold in town. Of course, there was no electricity or even a telephone. Kerosene lamps provided light and in an emergency Dad went by horseback to Frisco to use the telephone at the store.

A favorite Giberson family story pokes fun at Frisco's unpredictable weather. In 1912, the clan scheduled a July 4 picnic—only to be driven indoors by a blizzard. "The following day I was born in Frisco," Ann Giberson Dale wrote in her 1979 letter to the Frisco Historical Society.

Living on the ranch, now submerged by lake Dillon, Ann still heard the sound of the old narrow gauge as it swung out of the Canyon toward the tiny depot at the base of Mt. Royal.

> Speaking of the train, we could hear its whistle before it reached the Frisco depot which was at the other end of town. Riding the D & R G narrow gauge railway to Denver to visit grandmother was a days trip but an exciting one. People provided their own entertainment and the Denver Post was our link to the outside world.

Frisco's Dancing Feet

"I still love to dance," reminisced Ida Jane Linquist Murphy, daughter of Frisco's Swedish hotel proprietor. It was "our recreation—the Saturday night dance," she wrote in a 1984 letter. The dances rewarded residents after a week of hard work, and lit up their lives with foot-tapping music, friends, laughter and a midnight supper. Faye Turner Korthius remembered traveling three miles to the Dillon dance on skis one frigid winter night and returning "covered with frost from our breath."

> On one special occasion we skied down to Dillon to dance in the wintertime. Danced until one A. M. and skied home to Frisco arriving home about five A. M. and the temperature was 60 below zero. My grandmother said, "there will be no more of that."

Even the kids enjoyed these community get togethers. And they never missed the midnight meal! "When dances were held, the whole family went and when the children became sleepy, they would curl up on the benches and, covered by coats, sleep until refreshment time," Ann Giberson Dale recalls.

Frisco welcomed strangers to its social events. Easterner J. J. Gotch, who traveled to Frisco December 24, 1916 to meet a Professor Hennick, stayed at the old log Frisco Hotel. "We attended Christmas Eve festivities at the Community Hall nearby," Gotch wrote. (Profes-

4

sor Hennick, attempting to sell his Frisco mine to the Gotch's, showed them samples from his "fabulous mine chuck full of nuggets." Gotch wrote, "It was 'fool's gold'. He was accused of attempted fraud and we left for Leadville, Denver and back East on the Colorado & Southern.")

World Record on Prestrud's Ski Jump

Norwegian immigrant Peter Prestrud arrived in Frisco in 1910 to manage his father-in-law's investments in the King Solomon and Square Deal Mines. Discovering the mines to be less than thriving, he opened a grocery store and turned his leisure time attention to his favorite sport, ski jumping. Prestrud, a veteran of Norway's prestigious Holmenkollen ski meets, was an expert skier and jumper with an uncanny eye for a natural jumping hill.

Prestrud and his ski-happy pal, Eyvind Flood, built an ingenious ski jump at the Excelsior Mill in 1911, using the massive mine dump as a landing hill. William A. Wildhack remembered the jump site as "a 60 foot hill, with 35 to 40 foot jumps being typical and 50 to 60 foot jumps possible."

With Eyvind Flood, Prestrud became a master jump builder. Flood, who had come to the prim silver mining community of Sts. John in his teens, had shocked residents of nearby Montezuma with his speed and daring on skis. The pair began building a ski jump to end all ski jumps on the steep hillside above old Dillon. The Dillon Jump was completed in 1919. Word of this challenging new jump began to filter out among the small coterie of "yumpers," as the Scandinavian Jumping Team referred to themselves, around the West. In 1919, a ski jumper from Telemark, Norway, Anders Haugen, found his way over Loveland Pass to tiny Dillon and set a world distance record of 213 feet in March, 1919 on Peter Prestrud's jump. The big names in central Colorado ski jumping—Anders and Lars Haugen, Hans Hanson, Steamboat's Carl Howelson and of course, Eyvind Flood and Peter Prestrud—jumped on the Dillon Hill. Locals renamed it Prestrud Hill in 1954.

The jump site, located above the old town of Dillon, is above the present Dam Road near the scenic overlook. (Old Dillon, situated near the dam's "glory hole," occupied a site now beneath reservoir waters.) The cut for the jump's in-run can be seen high above the red rock outcroppings overhanging the Dam Road. The back street in Old Dillon, closed for jumping events, provided space to run out the skiers' jumps.

Almost singlehandedly, Peter Prestrud put Frisco on skis. The

Peter Prestrud

1883-1976

Norwegian immigrant Peter Prestrud left his vigorous stamp on Summit County and Colorado skiing. He and Steamboat's Carl Howelson are credited as "the fathers of ski competition" in this section of the Colorado Rockies. Numbered with the greats of Colorado winter sports, the early- day Frisco ski jumper excelled in competition and kindled his love for Nordic jumping and cross country among Coloradans. For his lifelong achievement, Prestrud was named to the Colorado Ski Hall of Fame in 1978, two years after his death on October 11, 1976 at age 93.

Newlyweds Peter and Alice Herseth Prestrud settled in Frisco in 1910, after meeting on an ocean liner during a trip from the U. S. to their native Norway. Prestrud received an appointment as Frisco postmaster in 1912, the year his first son, Lars, arrived. But a fire destroyed his postoffice- store in its first year of business. Prestrud managed the Excelsior Mine with Norwegian mining engineer, Eyvind Flood. The two built the Excelsior Mine ski jump in a steep crevice just northwest of the mine's Ten Mile Canyon portal location.

Edmund Couch, Jr., who nominated Peter Prestrud to the Ski Hall of Fame, wrote:

He had a keen sense for location of the various elements of a ski jump. In those days there were no guide line tables, and no analysis had been made of the mechanics of a ski jump. It amounted to finding a natural landing hill, usually a glacial or alluvial terrace—and even old landslides—then fitting in an in-run and take-off to the site. There was still some cut and try to get the desired effect. Surely the old mine dumps along the Ten Mile Canyon stirred his imagination when looking for a small ski jump site.

Prestrud later moved to Denver, but continued to compete at meets and to build ski jumps all over Colorado. In 1924, he snared the Colorado Amateur jump championship at Colorado Springs.

Skiers honored Prestrud in January, 1952 by establishing the Peter Prestrud trophy for the first annual Blue River Relay nordic race.

Peter Prestrud joined the ranks of men such as jumping comrade Anders Haugen, Aspen founder Walter Paepke and D.U.'s great ski coach Willie Schaeffler in the Ski Hall of Fame. Famous author-traveler, Lowell Thomas, spoke at the induction banquet.

A surgeon asked an 80-year old Peter Prestrud, entering a Denver hospital for an operation, to pinpoint his life's single most important event. Without hesitation, Prestrud replied, "When I pledged allegiance to the flag in Breckenridge, Colorado in 1915 and was given my citizenship papers."

young boys begged their parents for skis and practiced till they could handle Prestrud's jump. "Jim, Howard and Glenn Giberson skied and jumped at Dillon Hill. All the kids in town that skied used that jump," said Sue Giberson Chamberlain in a 1984 interview. Peter Prestrud organized ski competitions for local kids. From 1910 to 1923, he ran the events, judged and handed out prizes to the winners—medals, baseball gloves, jack knives, candy bars and gadgets that Prestrud persuaded local merchants to donate.

"Skis have largely supplanted both sleds and skates as a winter sport among young folks, and skiing parties are fast coming into favor," the March 28, 1914 *Blue Valley Times* reported. In winter, I went everywhere on skis," said early day Frisco resident Ida Jane Linquist Murphy. My first skis were barrel staves," remembered Bill Wildhack. "I slid down the snowbank outside our home."

Frisco's small fry took to downhill skiing with enthusiasm. A wonderful hill, now graded and gone, rose south on Second Avenue where the old school stands. Frisco schoolchildren tore into the contents of their lunch pails in a rush to be first on this hill at noon break. Again, after school, they skied and built a small jump for extra zest. All this body-crunching practice, in yesterday's toe-held longthong bindings, produced some parental gasps and an array of broken bones, injuring two Wortman boys and one Wiley and Wildhack. The school board added skiing to the curriculum before 1910. Ski instruction ceased during the Depression, but Summit school children enjoy ski classes winter afternoons today.

The natural moraine that traverses the southern end of Frisco provided two more ski hills where Frisco kids as late as the '50s learned to carve a turn. Piston Hill, behind the present postoffice, had its high point at the Frisco Street - Fourth Avenue intersection. Pavilion Hill rose on Granite between Third and Fourth. It would have become a town park with a pavilion today if a town clerk hadn't mistakenly sold the lots, according to a local legend passed along by Sue Chamberlain.

Adults caught the ski bug and strapped on the heavy spruce boards for winter outings. "...such a party... was held by Miss Hilda Baliff at the Baliff Ranch," said the March 28, 1914 *Blue Valley Times* commenting on one ski gathering. "Tip" Baliff, who had moved his blacksmith shop to Dillon in the 1880s, owned a ranch one and one-half miles east of Frisco.

Sweet Summer Days

Skiing helped Frisco's youngsters make it through all nine months of winter with a smile. When the Frisco Historical Society asked early day residents to write their memories, many recalled a childhood yearning for spring, a long-awaited event marked by the joy of finding the first wildflowers. Their joy was fleeting, for summer seemed to fly by:

> Summers were short and winters were long. My mother used to tell about my older sister as a little girl stomping out and pulling up Fireweed or what we used to call Summer Half Gone and in my mind's eye I can see a little girl with tears running down her cheeks desperately trying to stave off winter...
>
> 1979 Letter from Harold Deming

Summer did seem to hurry. And why not? Children's feet, light as whispers when freed from heavy galoshes, skipped away from the log schoolhouse in June to pluck wild strawberries, fish in beaver ponds and tramp along a crystal creek to a mountain picnic site.

"Our big thrill was to watch for the first signs of spring," wrote Faye Turner Korthius in a 1979 letter, "the first flower and the birds and chipmunks. It was really a delightful time."

> In the summertime, we would take a lunch and go up the canyon on berry picking trips. The black currants were delicious. Also, there was a man who had a truck who would come to town with fresh fruit and vegetables. They wouldn't last long as we were always hungry for anything green and especially fresh fruit was a luxury.

"My childhood memory is mostly of the beauty. I loved hiking in the mountains... In the spring, we watched for the first buttercups, bluebells and especially the 'Mayflowers'... Later gathering columbines by the armful," wrote Ida Jane Linquist Murphy.

Lars Prestrud remembered "huckleberry picking with Minnie Thomas and fishing in the ponds, Uneva Lake and Meadow Creek." Chick Deming wrote about his summertime fishing: "When I was a small boy growing up in Frisco... I remember fishing with a willow pole and a bent pin in the Tenmile creek by Olsons bridge. The Tenmile was a beautiful stream, clear and full of fish..."

Children climbed nearby peaks—Peak One for the aggressive and Mt. Royal for "tenderfeet." They picked golden pond lilies at Lily Pad Lake and caught frogs in the beaver ponds. They dreamed of adventure in the wild reaches of the wilderness Gore Range. Chick Deming said:

I remember, as a boy, the stories the old timers would tell of the wild Gore country just beyond Old Buffalo, a country of tall virgin timber with lakes and streams abounding with cutthroat trout, a wild canyon with deer, bear, blue grouse, Canadian lynx and the last hideaway for the lonesome old timber wolf. During the long winter months I would dream and plan of great explorations into the Gore country, of climbing Old Buffalo to see what was beyond the western horizon.

School bells ringing in a new term interrupted summer's freedom and joy. But Frisco students loved the one-room schoolhouse. Ann Giberson Dale described the long walk that ranch children faced each morning.

My sister Mildred and I walked to the one-room school in Frisco. There was nothing between the house and town except range cattle and the "Henderleiter Place" which had not been occupied for many years and was falling apart. To us it was a little spooky. We were well bundled up to protect us from the winter cold. The school was heated by a potbellyed stove (somewhat like the one in the depot.) There was one teacher and all grades were represented. If a minister happened to be visiting in town, church services were held in the school.

School teachers in the years before the sale of Ann's family ranch in 1919 were Alta Lynch, 1911; Georgia Condict, 1912; and Elsie Elsey, 1913-1917.

Influenza's Tragic Toll

The decade's most tragic event, for Frisco's children and their parents, was the 1918 influenza epidemic, a wildfire spread of lethal flu that swept Colorado, the nation and the world. The *Summit County Journal* devoted its entire front page to obituaries that year. Chris Cluskey, who lived part of his life in Frisco, worked as the Tiger mine camp's head teamster in 1918. He shouldered the sad task of driving flu victims' bodies to Breckenridge—sometimes as many as four per day. "Dr. Graham was our family doctor and he drove (to Frisco) to treat the family members who were ill during the severe flu epidemic of 1917-1918," wrote Ann Dale. Frisco's 1918 schoolmarm, Miss Richards, died at Christmastime, 1918, a flu victim. As late as February, 1920, influenza, coupled with its frequent mate, pneumonia, took the life of Friscoan John J. Deming.

Frisco marched into the "Roaring Twenties" to the beat of a differ-

ent drummer than most of the U. S. Almost every mine except
Masontown's Victoria had closed. Business had dwindled. Railroads
had pruned branch service. While Frisco's material wealth di-
minished, the town's spirit soared. Never did Frisco have more fun,
more community, more "big" family" brotherhood than those years
following the mining bubble's burst.

Hefty single pole assisted skiers in attempts to stop and turn on 15-lb. spruce skis,
Frisco's standard winter travel mode.

A Happy
Home Town

An elated Summit County crowd rallied round Peter Prestrud's Dillon Ski Jump for a February 29, 1920 jump tournament that made the movie newsreels. The *Summit County Star* dusted off its one and one-half inch "Second Coming" headline type to proclaim the news: A high-powered roster of professional and amateur jumpers, including world champion Anders Haugen, would compete on a jump layered with a foot of new-fallen snow to the cheers of a large crowd brought by special excursion trains. "A special train will take care of the Breckenridge crowd and extra coaches on the regular trains will be provided for the people of the Leadville and Ten Mile district," said the *Star*. The paper encouraged the crowds to buy their $1.10 round trip rail tickets before "the rush of train hour." Tents, erected at the ski jump base, provided warmth and refreshments. Admission cost $1, but "Getting In the Movies Will be Free," the paper announced. Universal Film Company had traveled to Summit County to film the event, to the giddy excitement of locals dreaming of being "discovered." "By taking in the tournament, you may accidentally get in the foreground of a moving-picture, and without extra charge, the photographer taking risks," an equally giddy *Summit County Star* said.

Local favorites Anders Haugen, former champion Henry Hall, Carl Howelson, and Hans Hansen numbered among the seven professional jumpers. Local competitor Peter Prestrud led a field of six Colorado amateurs. Their goal: To beat Anders Haugen's 1919 Dillon world record of 213 feet.

The crowd went wild in celebrating the winner's 214-foot jump. Their hero? Two-time winner Anders Haugen.

Summit County, seized with ski jumping excitement, sponsored a Summit Cup event for local jumpers, usually held during the Winter Sports Carnival. Robert Wiley walked away with the coveted cup by jumping 148 feet from the Dillon jump at a 1924 Summit Cup Tournament.

Frisco residents used skis not only at the Dillon and Excelsior Jumps, but also for transportation in an era when roads were never plowed. Horse drawn sleighs or cutters and skis carried people across the deep snows to their destinations—sometimes with hair-raising results. The Deming boys ran trap lines in the North Ten Mile and on Mt. Royal and Chief. Harold "Chick" Deming recalled:

> My older brother was caught in a snowslide and nearly lost his life. He lost one ski and had to strap a jack pine to his foot to get home. He always cautioned me about this area which layed on an old logging road cut into the side of the mountain and bare of timber. I was making a run on my trap line one day on snowshoes and was about half spooked of this area, a cornice had build up over the top of the cut and everything was just right for this slide to run. I hesitated for some time before attempting a crossing, finally I said what the hell and inched out into the open. I was about two thirds across the chute when I heard it break right under my snowshoes and gave a mighty leap to safety as it slipped away, it wasn't a big slide but it could have covered a guy up in a hurry, I know I was a mighty scared kid.

The U. S. Forest Service discourages today's cross-country skiers from using the scenic Ten Mile Canyon trail due to high avalanche danger. Early day residents faced the same hazard. The *Summit County Star* reported a 1920 accident typical of the old days and still a regular occurrence today.

> Archie Hogue, a tie cutter, was caught by a snow slide in the Ten Mile canon near Wheeler on Tuesday and shoved and rolled quite a distance down the steep and rocky western slope of the Ten Mile range. He was badly bruised and frigerated, but managed to dig himself out and go to his cabin. Here he was found by a patrolman of the Colorado Power company's transmission line, who tucked him into bed and then called Dr. C. E. Condon from Breckenridge. The latter dressed the man's bruises and gave him some stimulating medicine.

Avalanche Destroys Masontown

But the biggest snowslide of the 1920s roared off Mt. Victoria in 1926 to blow old Masontown to bits. Massive mine timbers were smashed to matchsticks in that avalanche. Its path down Victoria's northeast slope remains visible today. "We were awakened by the roar and the next morning Bob snowshoed up to Mason Town to look the slide over," said Chick Deming in a 1979 letter. "This is a good example of the power and destructive force in a major avalanche where huge timbers from the mill were completely destroyed.

Fred Echternkamp had worked Masontown's old Victoria Mine in 1916. After Prohibition had outlawed manufacture, transportation and sale of alcoholic beverages in 1920, bootleggers and moonshiners reputedly found deserted Masontown a haven for the washtub gin productions. Locals even whispered about a still.

But Providence works in strange ways. The moonshiners had disappeared by the time the avalanche smashed old Masontown. In an October 26, 1977 *Frisco News* article, Chick Deming's mother, Mrs. Nellie Deming Gurtler, told it this way:

> I came to Frisco in July of 1902. Masontown was started soon after. My brother, Whitney Rose, was the electrician there.

Avalanche demolished huge mine structure timbers as well as less sturdy log-frame buildings, reducing all to rubble in massive 1926 Masontown slide.

The machinery and supplies were hauled up to Masontown by Bill Staley. The boarding houses ran by George and Lillie Wortman, and at no time did they have more than 50 boarders.

There was a fiddler at Masontown. He played for the dances in Frisco. Mrs. Wortman said he fiddled backwards.

When the snowslide came down and wiped out all the buildings in the spring of 1926, none had lived there for years.

A pretty footpath leading from Frisco to the Masontown site makes a nice short hike for history buffs today. (For directions, see *The Summit Hiker* by Mary Ellen Gilliland.)

Mining's Last Gasp

Mining activity probably ceased before 1920 at Masontown. Popular Frisco square dance caller Charlie Rowe worked the Avalanche and the Rowe Tunnels on Chief Mountain during the '20s, according to Chick Deming, and the Frisco Tunnel, just above the Frisco Depot on Mount Royal was worked on and off till 1933. But mining had pretty much gasped its last by the 1920s. All that remained were mountains riddled by glory holes and tunnels and some grizzled old prospectors. One of these Frisco characters, Professor Oscar Hennick, holed up in an old cabin in the Ten Mile. He came to Frisco only when he ran out of grub. Mrs. Lizzie Wildhack, who ran the grocery, had some insight into the old codger's character. When the Professor advertised for a wife, a young lady from Kansas answered the ad, came to Colorado and married the old miner. Soon she appeared back in Frisco, a forlorn figure. Soft-hearted Mrs. Wildhack gave her train fare to return to Kansas. Hennick advertised again, but this time the lady, who arrived in town with two grown daughters, stayed overnight at the Frisco Hotel and had time to pick up the local scuttlebutt on her betrothed's notorious ways. When the unsuspecting Professor Hennick stepped off the C&S in Frisco to fetch his bride, she chased him with a club. Her two daughters behind her pommeled the Professor with brooms supplied by Mrs. Wildhack. They ran the disappointed groom out of town.

The hermit Hennick later died in his cabin. Some Frisco men went up the Canyon to check on him when his cabin light failed to come on for a few nights. The men had to shoot Hennick's dog to get inside to retrieve the body.

Frisco residents discussed the antics of local characters and other news items both at Wildhack's postoffice-store and at the town

John J. Deming

1874-1920

Nova Scotia-born John J. Deming joined his father, Elisha Deming, in Frisco in 1890, following a stint working in Leadville's silver-rich mines. (Family legend names the famous Little Johnny Mine.) Sixteen-year old John and his father homesteaded a large ranch in today's Frisco West. They later sold the homestead to Excelsior Mine owners, Ault and Wyborg.

When the pretty and accomplished Miss Nellie Rose took up residence in Frisco in 1902 as housekeeper for her brother, Bert, an Excelsior Mine electrician, Johnny Deming lost his heart. He married the 22-year old Kansas miss in a Christmas Eve, 1902 ceremony. The newlyweds lived in the Waterson house on Main Street.

John Deming spent a number of years in Frisco's timber industry, logging the forests near town. He also worked in local mines, including the Sky Pilot and the Surprise. "Dad was popular with the miners," Chick Deming remembered. The prospectors came to Deming moaning, "Johnny, I've got a toothache." Deming would give the miner a belt of whiskey, sit him down on a stump, and use forceps to extract the tooth. A rugged individual who loved the outdoors, John Deming measured up to most any challenge he faced. The man had a mischievous streak as well: Deming started the tradition of a patriotic dynamite blast on Piston Hill at 4 a.m. each July 4. His boys happily carried on, rattling Frisco's doors and windows, to the indignation of some less patriotic citizens.

Nellie and Johnny raised seven children, five boys and two girls. Their youngest, Chick, was only two in 1920 when a vigorous 46-year old John Deming succumbed to influenza-pneumonia, the killer epidemic that robbed so many local families of loved ones. The February 28, 1920 *Summit County Star* called Deming "a valued citizen and a man in the prime of life." Once more, the *Star* said, "death has deprived a large family of its provider and protector."

Nellie Deming "did about everything she could to keep the family intact," according to Chick Deming. She took in boarders, cooked for miners and did laundry. The older Deming boys went to work at an early age. The hard-working widow managed to raise a happy brood that hiked, hunted, fished and explored every inch of their wilderness "back yard." The Demings attended Frisco's log schoolhouse, worked in Frisco businesses and are buried in Frisco's cemetery. When Nellie died in 1967, Demings could point with pride to their contribution to Frisco's history since Grandfather Elisha's arrival in 1888.

spring, located between Fifth and Sixth on Galena. People from all over Frisco walked to the spring to haul back drinking and cooking water from the town's only pure water source. The spring provided "one of the main meeting places to discuss all topics of interest," according to Donald Kenneth Giberson.

A Peek at 1920s Home Life

The Turners lived at the the Huter home, a nice house with a fenced yard which they rented in the 1920s. Faye Turner Korthius wrote in 1979:

> We didn't have electricity or gas to cook by or inside plumbing... We had our Saturday night bath in the wash tub in the kitchen... We had a ways to go to the spring down the road and [carrying water] wasn't easy so we had one bath a week and then shared the bath water. We took turns being 'first' in the old wash tub.

Faye gave a vivid description of her home's rustic appointments:

> ...Our furniture consisted of orange crates or apple boxes. If we had an old iron bedstead with slats and coil springs, we were the elite. A table in the kitchen with chairs, nothing matched, of course, and a rocking chair a must. We had beds in every room in the house and my grandmother had several feather mattresses, which were really a delight and warm... To cook on a wood stove was a task, but we didn't mind.

Faye's family coped with the pitch black darkness of Frisco's unlit streets by devising an ingenious lantern.

> The streets were rough and no arc lights to let you know where you were. We made our own lanterns if we had to go out after dark, which consisted of a large can, generally a Karo syrup pail, with a piece of wire for a handle and a candle inside for light. It was amazing how well you could see with this contraption.

Indoors, families used candles and oil lamps, according to Sue Giberson Chamberlain, then later gas lamps that gave much better light. Life on the Giberson ranch meant more chores for kids than town children had. "We had a lot of fun, but we didn't have that much time to play," Sue recalled in a February 16, 1978 *Summit Sentinel* article. "There was a lot of work to do on a ranch. We couldn't just run around all the time... There were cows to milk, hay to put up and guests to take care of. My parents were very hospitable and it seems like someone was always staying with us." Later, when Sue was a teenager, she delivered milk to dairy customers in town. "I remember delivering to Mrs. Staley. Milk sold for 10 cents a quart, and heavy whipping cream sold for 25 cents a pint." Sue's mother, Mollie, also churned butter and made delicious, rich ice cream for special customers.

Preparing for Frisco Winters

Both ranch and town families stockpiled food for winter in quantities that today seem prodigious. Frisco rancher Howard Giberson remembers his family's pantry bulging with "a ton of potatoes, 1,000 pounds of flour, cases of canned peas, corn and beans, and huge quantities of dried fruit ordered from Montgomery Wards." The Gibersons canned pork in its lard and cured hams, made sausage and scrapple. They hung meats in a shed outside to freeze.

"We would buy in large quantities, cases of canned goods, one hundred pounds of flour, lard, sugar, coffee were the staples," said Faye Turner Korthius. "Some things were hard to store. Meat was a problem. Some folks could can it, but it wasn't easy, especially on a wood stove. We ate some fish and venison when we could get

Frisco summers found families stocking up for winter. Here, Louis and Lizzie Wildhack pose with son, Bill, and daughter, Mattie.

it and it was in season."

While food storage threatened to crowd out the family within, the wood pile grew to enormous proportions outside. The Deming family jerryrigged a motorized saw that turned out a winter wood supply in three days.

> Preparing for winter in those days took a lot of effort. We had to haul in enough dry wood to run from October through May and this would have to be sawed into stove lengths. We had an old 1925 Overland stripped down that we would set on steel wheels that were belted to a circular saw, after we got the old car set up on the wheels and fired up 2 of us would buck the logs into the saw and one kid would throw the blocks as they were sawed off, in about 3 days of steady sawing we would have a pile at least as big as the house and everyone would breathe a sigh of relief knowing we would make it through the winter.

> Some of our neighbors weren't so lucky and would saw all of their wood by hand with a one man crosscut saw. There was very little money in the county and very little work.

Old Frisco also worked in winter to prepare for summer. Young William Wildhack cut huge blocks of ice from local beaver ponds to store in sawdust for summer refrigeration use. His favorite, "the Kids' Ponds," bordered the railroad tracks near Bill Thomas' ranch. Young Wildhack usually hired a local rancher with a sled to help him haul the ice. One year, he and his girlfriend, Marty, devised a less costly method. "I would get four or six blocks at one time and put them in the old touring car I had and bring them home to the ice house," he said.

No matter how hard Friscoans worked, they still had the energy to dance till sunrise. "I recall the square dances at the Town Hall," wrote Donald Kenneth Giberson. "These dances would often last till daylight, if the wood would last for the heating stove in the corner of the Hall." Ike Rouse still fiddled, Mary Rouse chorded on the piano and Ben Staley called. Mrs. Lillie Wortman, who often hosted midnight suppers at the Frisco Hotel, became one of Frisco's beloved women, with Mrs. Mallory, the midwife who assisted so many Frisco babies into the world during home births, running a close second.

Frisco's children had a happy time during the 1920s. Lars Prestrud reminisced about his first motorcycle ride, perched behind Henry Heckman on the bumpy dirt road to the King Solomon Mine.

Frisco's much-loved Minnie Thomas took the Prestrud kids huckleberry picking, and the Giberson family loved to visit her home at Bill's Ranch. "To entertain the kids, Minnie would play the old Edison phonograph," Ken Giberson recalled. "The records were round like a cylinder or barrel, with open ends. We thought the music was great." His sister, Sue, remembered the fun of pasting up pictures Minnie had cut from magazines.

A Venerable Professor

Just as special as Minnie Thomas, was Frisco's venerable 1920s schoolmaster, Professor I. O. Jones. The frail professor's physical strength had waned enough that the big boys had to haul him through the deep snows to school on a sled. But the schoolteacher's strong spirit permeated the classroom. His nine students in 1920-21 learned kindness, respect, independent thinking, self-determination and an enduring love of learning. Professor Jones rewarded good work by allowing children to read from his cherished "Book of Knowledge," according to former student William A. Wildhack. When the aged Professor first arrived in town, Wildhack's mother, Lizzie, met him at the train station dressed in her Sunday-best white gloves and hat, a sign of deference to his learning that both parents and children continued. In 1923, another man taught in the one-room schoolhouse. "Our teacher was Earl Pemberton who taught all eight grades and I recall there were only ten children in school," wrote Faye Korthius. The Frisco school board hired Pemberton because he could teach ninth and tenth grades. When Bill Wildhack grew old enough to attend high school in Breckenridge, his family was "too poor to go anywhere" so Pemberton taught tenth grade. "The next year, he taught me tenth grade over again with different subjects. It wasn't too good, but it was school," said Wildhack.

While 1920s Frisco tightened its financial belt with a spare town treasury balance in 1927, and the business of living without gas, electricity, running water or indoor bathrooms might seem bleak, Frisco's 138 residents managed to live lives full of richness, warmth and happiness. When Wall Street crashed in 1929 and ruined financiers jumped from skyscraper windows in despair, Frisco found itself with no money to lose and no window high enough to cause more than injured pride. And though Frisco faced the spectre of hard times as the Depression years made their grim debut, the town's already-poor populace didn't really notice any differences.

CHAPTER 7

Sweet and Simple Years

God love these mountain women anyway,
Said Mr. Probus. Not to say they're fair
Or sleek with oils, for woodsmoke in the hair
And sagebrush on the fingers every day
Are toughening perfumes, and the sunstreams flay
Too dainty flesh. But what remains is rare,
Like mountain honey to the mountain bear.
He finds his relish in a rough bouquet.

Days when their wash is drying, off they'll go
And fish the beaver ponds. Hell or high water
They'll wade the slues in sunburnt calico
Playing a trout like some old sea-king's daughter.
(Belle Turnbull, *The Tenmile Range*)

"Old Man Moore bought that building for 98 cents, plus 2 cents tax, and paid a dollar to put a lock on the door!" That's how longtime resident C. S. Thompson capsuled Frisco's economic low in the 1930s. His remark concerned the sale of the spacious, sturdily-built Curtin railroad boarding house, located two miles from Frisco at the Ten Mile Canyon rail camp. (The structure, the only one around that boasted a plastered interior, ended up as a chicken house on the Ruth property—another kind of boardinghouse.) Frisco lots sold for bottom-of-the-barrel prices—$5 (buy three and get a fourth lot free!) Eighteen hardy souls populated 1930 Frisco, according to the *Colorado Yearbook 1937-38 Gazetter*. The town coffers rattled with a scant $56.13 in 1934. To make bad matters worse, Frisco lost its telephone service in 1935.

One resident said it this way: "Everyone knew what everyone else had—nothing!'

One Friscoan who ran short on cash also ran long on creativity. William "Bill" Thomas, who with his brother Walter, owned 146-acre Bill's ranch just south of Frisco, sat down one day in 1930 to write a letter. With Walter buzzing ideas in his ear, Bill penned a unique sales letter—an offer to 100 selected individuals for a free ranch lot—no strings attached. To names he carefully selected from *The Denver Post*, the dairy rancher wrote:

Mr. Man:

Here IS something. Something, actually for nothing. A dandy cabin site absolutely free. A site that many tell me should sell for upwards of two hundreds dollars—and which might sell for such a figure in the near future. For these cabin sites are located in what thousands have acclaimed as the prettiest and most picturesque spot in the entire Rocky Mountain region. A spot dotted with clear, cold mountain springs; cool, shady pines; and carpeted with columbines, wild roses and many other beautiful wild mountain flowers.

You see, it is this way: I am long on land and short on good neighbors. And I would like to get a little sort of a summer resort started on my place. So, after Mrs. Thomas and I talked it over, we decided to simply give away a few—perhaps a dozen—of these choice cabin sites to folks who will, in our estimation, turn out to be good friends...

Bill's rationale? If people built cabins on the ranch, he'd have a guaranteed market for his milk, butter and cream. Sounds crazy today, but in cash-tight Depression days, Bill's plan made a strange kind of sense.

The first—and for a while the only—taker was an Evangelical minister from Denver, Robert D. Dexheimer. According to his daughter, Roberta Dexheimer Fiester, Rev. Dexheimer waved the letter before his family at the dinner table, gave them a lecture on how you never get something for nothing and said, "Let's go."

"Frisco was just a wide spot in the road," laughed Roberta Fiester. "Wildhacks had the postoffice and the Frisco Hotel was there. Papa went over and got a room—just one room because it was during the Depression—for my mother and grandmother." The rest of the family planned to spend the night in an old barn west of the hotel. First they cooked a few cans of beans over a fire for dinner. "We were camping right on Main Street, but that didn't bother anybody because Main Street had only a few dilapidated buildings. There were no street lights. The stars came out, more stars than I had ever seen in my life."

Soon, however, the celestial display disappeared behind a blanket of thunderheads. The campers retreated to the barn to escape the deluge—and found it damp, reeking of its rodent inhabitants and freezing cold. Roberta's father wrapped heated stones from the campfire in burlap to warm the family's feet, but the ancient burlap began to smoke, filling the barn with a revolting odor. "Sleep was impossible," Roberta remembered.

But morning—"a glorious morning"—came. Early day Frisco, its beauty undisturbed by construction and highway bulldozers, delighted the Dexheimers and their companions, Mr. and Mrs. Maddy who had camped at the then-stunning Canyon mouth.

The party crossed Jud Creek (also known as "Jug") and Miners Creek enroute to Bill's Ranch, muttering, "What can be wrong with this place that they're giving it away?"

But the wildflower-dotted aspen and pine forest cut by tumbling Miners Creek, was alive with deer, beaver, coyote, porcupine—and Bill's friendly burros, "Popcorn" and "Peanuts." It proved to be a dream come true.

> My father had his pick of all the land on the ranch. Mr. Maddy took the lot adjoining him on the north. Upon return to Denver my father announced his find to the congregation of his Denver church and Mr. McKee (Mac as he was fondly known here in the area), Mrs. Mix who built a lodge with adjoining cabins, the Ninnemans, Niemoths and DeSellems all came up here. The 100 letters Bill sent out were ignored, but Papa was a great salesman and he soon had Bill's Ranch well populated.

Only one other letter recipient, a Mr. Boggs from Kansas, replied to Bill Thomas' incredible letter.

Bill's Ranch, Frisco's first subdivision and its first second-home development, emerged a success. Today's town planners would throw up their hands at Bill's hodgepodge of jumbled odd-size lots, without road access, and its collection of Depression days slab-log cabins. But homeowners improved their buildings when better times arrived. And the Ranch became the scenic home of Frisco's historic and hospitable Ophir Lodge.

In July, 1931, the elderly Jane Thomas sold Frisco's well-known Thomas Hotel to Evelyn Mix. The 1879-built stagecoach stop, originally The Leyner Hotel, gained new life as Ophir Lodge, a cozy retreat for vacations, weddings and parties beside a pretty man-made lake on Bill's Ranch.

Pearl Mix Garvin, and her husband, Duane, celebrated their wedding at the finished Lodge in 1933. She detailed the historic building's move:

> In the late summer and fall of 1931 the hotel building was carefully dismantled. Each log was numbered and all useable materials were hauled to the ranch site by Bill Thomas, using a wagon and team of horses. The first floor of the hotel building was used for the Lodge livingroom; the upper story, built adjacent to the livingroom, became the diningroom, and the two rooms were connected by a screened porch. All room partitions were eliminated, leaving large, open rooms. The walls of the livingroom and diningroom were constructed from the original hand-hewn timbers, approximately 12" square.
>
> Ophir Lodge was opened to tourists and vacationers June 1, 1932 and continued in operation until 1958. Evenings were spent in the livingroom visiting, playing games and singing. The granite-faced fireplace was built from rocks gathered at the King Solomon Mine dump. Rocks for the chimney were gathered from the surrounding hillsides.

Reverend Dexheimer often conducted Sunday evening services at Ophir Lodge. Mrs. Mix often invited the family for meals and an evening of singing by the piano in front of the big stone fireplace. Except for misadventures—such as the time a large honey-colored bear robbed the hard-up Dexheimer family's outdoor "California cooler" of a ham, a longhorn cheese and a slab of bacon—life on Bill's Ranch proved idyllic.

Hoover Dinners

Despite its simplicity, life in Frisco remained equally blissful. Elizabeth Mumford Peterson described the tiny community's happy "Hoover Dinners." "Everyone who came brought what food they could spare and it was cooked in a big iron pot on the huge cast iron stove. My Aunt Mary (Mary E. Ruth) would bake bread for the dinners. I always enjoyed eating at the enormous table."

When early-day Frisco hosted a potluck or picnic, *everyone* came. "Everyone in town was invited. No one was left out," Sue Giberson Chamberlain related. Her brother, Howard Giberson, listed Uneva Lake Falls and the Soda Springs near Montezuma as Frisco's favorite picnic spots. Picnickers brought plenty of lemons to make fizzy lemonade at the soda springs. Potato salad, relishes and ham provided a preliminary to the day's treat: Rich homemade ice cream and freshly-baked cake. The ice cream arrived in its own freezer, well-wrapped in gunny sacks to stay cold.

During this time novelist Helen Rich and her inseparable friend, poet Belle Turnbull, lived in Frisco. They later became Breckenridge's well-known "French Street Ladies," a literary pair held in high esteem. Their poetry and prose on life beneath the Ten Mile range gained a national audience.

Another blueblood adopted into Frisco's homespun family was Susan Emery Badger.

A fugitive from her aristocratic New England family, Miss Badger came to Frisco to free herself from the fetters of social rank and the rigors of life among the high-born. "Until I came here to Summit County," she said in an *Empire* magazine interview, "the only accomplishment I could call my own was the ability to knit a Kitchener toe. I was known solely as 'the granddaughter of' or 'the daughter of.' Up here," she declared, "I am me."

The Maine governor's granddaughter shed her rigid Republican background. She cast off her Episcopalian mindset. Then, in 1936, she became Summit County's Welfare Department director. The job put the proper Miss Badger in touch with raw human problems—and her response made her the person she wanted to be. Susan Emery Badger wangled W.P.A. jobs for unemployed Depression-era laborers, drove Frisco youngsters over hairpin-strewn Hoosier Pass for eye doctor appointments, married young adults as justice of the peace and buried a baby in a handmade casket. She played a crack game of poker with cigar-puffing male pals and read bedtime stories to Frisco's children from her front porch rocker. In a near quarter century of service to Summit County, Susan Emery Badger wore the badges of justice of the peace, deputy sheriff, police matron and humane officer. Throughout those years, Miss Badger lived in an unassuming log house on Galena Street that she purchased in 1935.

High Times for Frisco's Youth

Hard times failed to squelch the enthusiasm of Frisco's youth for their mountain playground. Donald Kenneth Giberson described this free-ranging fun:

> The Deming boys and the Giberson boys were very close friends, and the Deming boys spent considerable time at our ranch. Often Chick Deming and I would take off hiking for 2 or 3 days, with only a fishing pole, rifle and blanket. We'd often go over on the Gore, climb Buffalo mountain, see

Wheeler Lakes or Lost Lake up Officer's Gulch, or just bum around at the head of North Ten Mile, Meadow Creek or Willow Creeks.

Nor did hard times dampen a young man's romantic notions. Ken Giberson recalled his efforts to impress Frisco's young ladies.

I worked one summer for Mr. Wildhack, owner of the Frisco store and also the Postmaster. I did some prospect work for him on Dickey Mountain. We didn't find any ore, but he loved to prospect. During this period, I courted his niece, Lillian Woods, who worked in the store. I didn't like to go in the store without buying something, so my mother would let me buy a $.35 pound of coffee, which included a drinking glass. We generated a cupboard full of drinking glasses that summer.

In 1938, Giberson lost his heart to Burdena White, a pretty miss visiting the MacMasters family at their cabin just northeast of town.

Trapping provided Depression-days livelihood for Frisco's Deming boys.

Susan Emery Badger

1886-1972

This "silk-stocking pioneer" arrived in Colorado Springs on a stretcher in 1916, seriously ill with tuberculosis. Her cure may have come from the dry Colorado air, but more probably from the inviting Colorado mountains, which beckoned her to get out of bed and begin a new life.

Slowly, Susan Emery Badger did. After a 14-year stint as headmistress of the San Luis academy for girls, a carriage trade boarding school (1920-1934), Miss Badger packed up her Model A Ford and disappeared into a gap in the mountains, leaving her upper-crust life behind.

"She camped in a tent up the North Ten Mile by the waterfall," said Cap Thompson, recalling Miss Badger's earliest years in Frisco. She boarded with Otillia Olson in 1934, then bought her small, weathered, log house at 407 Galena Street in 1935. She lived there for 35 years, pumping water from a well, chopping her own wood and boasting of "the most distinguished privy in town." Her arrival coincided with the walloping 1935-36 winter, when all the passes closed January 25 to April 22. That year, and many winters to follow, Miss Badger parked at Ken Chamberlain's Main Street garage and waded through deep snow to her home.

She soon landed a job as County Welfare Director, with no experience or credentials except a clergyman's letter praising her moral character and a merchant's avowal that she paid her bills on time. The middle-aged Miss Badger dove into the job that assured her, by virtue of its paltry salary, of comparative poverty. Her listening ear, her belief that men want work, not welfare, and her cheerful willingness to tackle any job earned her "hands off" respect from superiors.

"While eccentric might not be the word for Miss Badger," Phyllis LaBarr wrote in a *Women as Tall as Our Mountains* profile, "she certainly had not been homogenized out of her individuality." Miss Badger provided a salty study in contrasts. On the one hand, she upheld the strictest of social proprieties. She always wore a hat, with a hat pin, over her long hair done up in a French roll. She had a "work hat," a black tam, for casual wear. The only time anyone ever saw Miss Badger without a hat, Susie Thompson remembers, was during World War II when news came that Mary Ruth's son, Bernard, was missing in action. A hatless Miss Badger rushed to the Ruth home to comfort Mary. Miss Badger understood grief. Her fiance had died shortly before their wedding day during her youth in Maine. Susan Emery Badger granted the privilege of first name familiarity to a select few, dressed in an elegant Eastern wardrobe, made a ritual of afternoon tea and "always smelled of lilacs."

On the other hand, Miss Badger smoked ("but not around us because she connected us with the church," said Lola Mae Bristol) and maintained a mildly shocking lifestyle. Ed Funk wrote in the January 5, 1978 *Summit County Journal*:

> During the evenings, a resident of her hometown of Frisco could find her in her nightgown and robe lounging on her front porch, sipping a glass of whiskey and enjoying the mountain air. Inside, she had a royal flush that she had held in a poker game framed and hanging on her wall.

She loved children and animals. Every child who grew up in Frisco over three decades remembers his or her excited search for the first May flower. Miss Badger awarded the lucky finder five cents in the early days and 25 cents by the 1950s and '60s. She tutored the Tutt children at Uneva Lake and Russell Tutt remembers her arriving on his birthday with a special gift. A few hours later, the other young Tutts would also receive presents, so they would not feel left out.

"Dinah," Miss Badger's registered Scotty dog went everywhere with her mistress. Susan Badger installed a board bench above the back seat of her car so Dinah could ride in style. She often said, "The more I see of men, the more I love my dog."

A family of baby squirrels once took a shine to playing in the Bristol home, entering through a skylight. The Bristols remember an early Sunday morning when the boys roused the family with their ruckus in chasing the squirrels. "I was chasing these squirrels out of the house one day and up a tree," said Lola Mae Bristol. Miss Badger, wearing the badge of humane officer, came across the street from her home and warned Mrs. Bristol in no uncertain terms to stop harassing the squirrels.

Susan Badger, who once cut up her best white satin pajamas to line the casket of a poor family's baby scalded to death, died herself on March 27, 1972. Two broken hips, in 1964 and 1967, forced her to accept care in the Fairplay nursing home the last few years of her life. Her close friends, Cap and Susie Thompson, visited her there, once bringing from her home by request a treasured gold ring that was, long ago, to be Miss Badger's wedding ring.

When I would go after the milk cows in the evening, I would select our prettiest horse, put on chaps and spurs, coil up the lariat, and ride by the MacMasters cabin. I would wave to Burdena, but normally she'd ignore me and slip into the cabin. Later that summer, a town picnic was held, and I arranged to sit by Burdena during the games. We were married three years later.

The Frisco boys didn't always demonstrate this gallant behavior. A favorite Deming boys antic involved blasting Frisco's sleeping citizens out of bed at dawn on July 4 by detonating dynamite on Piston Hill. "Often, the Giberson boys would help," wrote Ken, "particularly if the July 3rd dance at Slate Creek broke up by daylight."

When Halloween came, Depression-decade Frisco kids had to forego the "treats," but they made up for it by indulging in tricks.

For 182 days of every year, Frisco's one room schoolhouse put a lid on these high energies. In September, 1938, however, teachers and school board, not keyed-up students, erupted in a blow-out that caused a school closing. As Providence would have it, schoolteacher Kenneth Caldwell happened to visit Frisco the weekend following the Friday closure. A friend who had a sister in Frisco had suggested they drive up to visit. The community gathered that Saturday evening for a house-warming at the Allen's, who had moved the office from the Excelsior Mine to Frisco as their new home. (The red building still stands on Galena Street today.) All the talk that evening centered on the school situation: The board president had resigned, the teacher quit and the future of Frisco's empty schoolhouse looked grim.

"Ken's a teacher," the friend suggested. "Ask him."

Next day the school board met and hired Kenneth Caldwell.

"I rang the school bell on Monday morning. I think there were fewer than 10 students altogether," Caldwell said.

Frisco's Musical Schoolmaster

That's how Frisco's beloved teacher began. His 20-year teaching career in Frisco and later Dillon spanned a generation, bridging a gap between old-time Frisco's one-room schoolhouse and a new educational world that demanded Frisco's three present schools. Kenneth Caldwell's greatest gift to Frisco would be his music, from piano lessons for little people to the creation of a community orchestra.

Caldwell's most immediate problem in 1938, however, was not

music, but money. "I came to Frisco with my last $10 and spent some of that on gas," he remembered. Caldwell had to pay a $5 fee for a Colorado teacher's certificate and didn't have the cash. Susan Badger, a 1938 Frisco school board member, gave Caldwell the necessary $5.

Even today he wants you to know—he paid it back.

"I was in seventh heaven except for the salary," Caldwell recalled. "The pay was $100 monthly. The board never raised the amount in four years teaching at Frisco."

Caldwell thrived on the dynamic of the one-room Frisco schoolhouse. The older children took responsibility to help the little ones and also included the younger ones in their games. "That was a nice feature in one-room schools," he said. "If a small child had a splinter or got hurt in another way, an older student would help."

Kenneth Caldwell loved the one-room schoolhouse. "I liked knowing the kids well. You can do quite a few creative things with a group of children of different ages. There was a place in our country's history for the one-room school. It really played a part," said Caldwell, who taught in an Illinois one-room school prior to his Frisco post.

Elizabeth Mumford Peterson wrote, "I don't remember reading, writing or arithmetic, but we had an orchestra. I played the triangle."

Teaching children piano after school and on weekends prompted an interest in music among Kenneth Caldwell's pupils. Kids, excited to play, dragged in discarded instruments from home and learned. Soon Caldwell had a pint-sized orchestra on his hands. Adults, some of them trained musicians, joined their tuned-in kids and a 16-member community orchestra emerged, performing several concerts a year. Their success encouraged a group of talented adults to gather with Caldwell to form a Frisco players troupe. Ken Giberson, Howard and Lura Belle Giberson, Harold Deming, Jean Deberry, Steve and Jane Guthrie, along with Ken Caldwell and his wife Maxine, presented their wacky musical variety productions in Frisco between 1938 and 1942. They decided to take one successful show to Slate Creek. "The light plant at Slate Creek broke down, so we had to use lanterns," Lura Belle Giberson chuckled. She played a Negro woman, her skin blacked with burnt cork. The light was so poor, however, she faded into the dark background. The hooting audience began to see Lura Belle more clearly during her washer-woman scene. She dunked her hands in the soapsuds to scrub and they came out gleaming white. Actors joined the audience in a good guffaw.

Kenneth Caldwell's musical talent blessed Frisco in uplifting ways. He played for church services and his wife, Maxine, sang. "She never missed a Sunday," Friscoans remember. After decades with no regular religious service, Frisco now had a church of sorts, housed in the old log schoolhouse. Pastor Ord Morrow preached. Frisco remained so thankful at having church services that townsfolk could forgive Kenneth Caldwell's passion for playing the piano "in the middle of the night."

End of an Era

Wildhack's postoffice and store changed hands in 1935 when Louis A. Wildhack sold the 1880s building to Guy Cannam. Frisco's longtime postmaster had resigned. His gregarious wife, Lizzie, closed her cash register for the last time. Local children, who always received candy from her when the monthly bill was paid, moaned. Frisco's gathering place moved into a new era. Miss Badger had come every evening to pass the time with Wildhacks. For some, the visit to Wildhack's store highlighted a day. The old postoffice had always hummed with conversation at train time, twice daily in the 1930s. The morning train from Leadville arrived, the Lord willing, at 10:30 a.m. Postmaster Wildhack pushed his two-wheeled cart up to the depot at Mt. Royal's base and picked up mail bags and shipments. Young William Wildhack remembered struggling on the rough gravel track with the balky cart. When the cart returned, residents waited while Wildhack sorted mail and stuffed postal boxes.

"At 4:12 was the time the train from Denver was supposed to come. We had to wait if the train was late, as it often was," said Bill Wildhack. "In winter time, of course, we pulled the mail on sleds and when the weather was such that neither sled nor cart was appropriate, we had trouble."

C & S Shutdown Sequesters Frisco

The Colorado & Southern finally discontinued service to Summit County in 1937, a move that ended more than a half-century of colorful high country railroad history. Despite the hazards of keeping track open during heavy winter snows, avalanche damage, tortuous high mountain pass routes and rail accidents, the C&S had linked Frisco to the outside world with a vital lifeline.

As the C&S took up its wooden ties in 1937, Friscoans made a mad dash to retrieve the lumber for firewood. When they took a deep breath and looked around to survey county roadways, residents reacted with horror. Loveland Pass, a rough track from Georgetown, was, the Gibersons said, "a way through, but no road, nobody drove a car on it." Work crews completed grading Loveland for auto travel in 1939 and the 11,992-foot route served hardy motorists. Hoosier, another Continental Divide pass, provided access to Denver via South Park, but the exposed, above-timberline route often closed in winter. The long way to Denver, north via Kremmling, used Berthoud Pass, where a mammoth mud hole threatened to swallow vehicles.

There were no paved highways, only rough, rocky roads.

Just staying home began to look better to Frisco residents in the late '30s when Depression-era W.P.A. projects spruced up the town. In February, 1937 the town board started scraping up cash for materials to repair the town hall with W.P.A.-supplied labor. Frisco commissioned Miss Badger as a committee of one to approach Leadville's Public Service Company about lights for Frisco. Miss Badger, duly reported the reply. "Yes. And the cost will be $1400." The

Friscoans supplemented winter railroad travel between towns with horse-drawn sleigh and ski transportation. After the rails shut down, citizens required the services of plows like this one to keep roads open.

board sighed and tabled the project.

Frisco lacked utilities, but townspeople plumbed the community's greatest resources, its wild, rugged "back yard," the majestic Gore range wilderness. Mildred Rutherford, who lived on Prestrud's old Meadow Creek Ranch known in the '30s as the Huter Ranch, wrote of her father's activities in the Gore, "Dad trapped marten in the cliffs between Buffalo Mountain and Red Peak. He... stayed overnight in the Hawes cabin... on the headwaters of Maryland Creek. Snow was often 60 feet deep in the canyons."

Elizabeth Mumford Peterson explored closer to Frisco, but enjoyed nature's beauty as much.

> My father, Russel Mumford, and I did a lot of walking in the evening. We would walk toward Rainbow Lake and bring back down-timber for fire wood. On walks to the lily ponds across the river you could sometimes see a mother bear and her cubs. Walking up the North Ten Mile was more exciting because there was good chance you could hear a cougar scream. I liked scrambling around the King Solomon tailings and finding pretty rocks.

The district's undisturbed natural beauty began to disappear, however. Harold Deming chronicled the beginnings of change:

> In the late twentys and early thirties [Climax Mine] tailings were dumped directly into the Tenmile, and this killed nearly all of the aquatic life, vegetation, fish and insects, leaving a fine grained smelly compound of waste rock and chemicals coating everything in and along that once beautiful stream.

CHAPTER **8**

Sunrise for a Sleepy Town

When Edwin E. and Esther Swanson first followed the dirt road over Loveland Pass, through old Dillon and on to Frisco, they found a tiny town with "12 permanent residents, plus several summer-time people." Just before sunset, Bill Thomas walked his cows along Main Street, "back to his ranch after a day's grazing in the nearby meadow," the Swansons said. Soon kerosene lamps glowed in cabin windows.

People gathered at Chamberlain's Frisco Cafe, where they ordered a cup of coffee for five cents, and if pocketbooks allowed, a dish of ice cream. They passed the evening in conversation and laughter flowed out into a quiet Main Street lit by a canopy of stars.

Frisco, in the year 1940, shrank to nearly a shadow. Cap and Susie Thompson, summer residents in the late '30s, remembered only five of six families that stuck out the Frisco winter. The Thompsons themselves established year-round residence in 1942. But Frisco's flicker of life did not snuff out. The War and post-War years fanned the town's tiny flame with new faces, some temporary such as the Tenth Mountain Division soldiers, some longterm like the Robert Footes, the Harold Thompsons, the Bill Fails, and Ralph Porterfields.

Frisco in the '40s finally moved into the twentieth century. In July, 1940, the town granted Public Service Company of Leadville a franchise to provide the town with electricity. Though tight-fisted town board members failed to fund street lights, homeowners rejoiced at placing gas lamps on a shelf. (Typical home lighting, crude at first, featured a single bulb hanging from a cord in the center of a room.)

Just after electric power lit up Frisco, the power of the Lord, in the person of Reverend Harold Thompson, arrived in town. Assisted by a single volunteer, Harold Thompson built a homely log chapel, a long peak-roofed structure that looks like the handiwork of pioneers. (The building still stands alongside the alley between Main and Granite near Sixth Avenue.) Rough handhewn benches and a sawdust floor added more convincing evidence to the pioneer image. The chapel cost next to nothing because a friendly U. S. Forest Service ranger pointed Thompson to a timber stand near Keystone that he could fell for free. The overjoyed preacher grabbed his saw and raced out to cut the stand in 35-degree below zero weather and knee-deep snow.

Meanwhile, like the itinerant preachers of old, Reverend Thompson circuit-preached at Summit's far-flung communities— Montezuma, the Civilian Conservation Corps camp at Keystone, Dillon, Kokomo and Climax. By the mid-forties, 25 to 30 attended church in Thompson's living room and in the town hall. The Reverend began to contemplate a real church building.

In 1947, volunteers poured a foundation for a new Rocky Mountain Bible Church, a construction project that required "the Lord's good time" to complete. Neighbor Helen Foote watched the snail's pace progress from her window. "I'll never forget seeing Hattie Lund up there on the roof nailing down boards." An icy wind blew that autumn, and the widowed Mrs. Lund had passed her 70th birthday.

The frame structure did open for worship in September, 1953. Today the Rocky Mountain Bible Church awaits the completion of a third church building.

Frisco's sparse population, coupled with World War II's outbreak, forced closing of the 40-year old log schoolhouse during the war years, 1942-1947. Teacher Ken Caldwell took his little flock to the two-room Dillon school. He remained there many years, seeing growth that brought a new gymnasium with a "wonderful stage" and "a hardwood floor polished to a shine." All this, and a central heating system too!

The Frisco school re-opened in 1947 under Mrs. Armstrong's direction, then Earl Baker taught from 1948 till 1950.

In 1947, five-year old Patty Foote visited school. The precocious Patty sat at her desk reading a science book— until nine-year-old Loren Thompson reached over and turned the book right side up. Kenneth Caldwell later became county schools music teacher, traveling from morning teaching in Breckenridge to Kokomo, Dillon, Slate Creek and Lakeside in the afternoons. When school finished for the day he gave piano lessons. Caldwell arrived to teach Patty Foote music on the family's 100-year old pump organ. Helen Foote remembered:

> Kenneth, with pencil in hand, was tapping the organ and

counting "1, 2, 3, 4" over and over. Brother Bobby, who was learning to count, came to his mother and said, "I feel so sorry for Mr. Caldwell for he can only count to four."

War brought changes not only for Frisco schoolchildren, but also for postal patrons. While the 1941 postmaster Edwin "Elmer" Swanson stood sorting the mail, he picked out his own draft notice. When Swanson went off to war, his wife Esther Swanson took over as postmaster. Her appointment came June 24, 1942. After only a few months, Esther Swanson had to move to Denver. Frisco faced the loss of its 63-year old postoffice.

Mary Ruth came to the rescue. Though Breckenridge-born Mary Ellen Cluskey Ruth lived with her husband Bill at Uneva Lake, the couple had a house in Frisco. The postoffice moved from its decades-old station at 510 Main Street to Mary Ruth's remodeled coal shed, a salvation for Frisco's postoffice. Mary faithfully traveled from Uneva Lake every day to sort letters, post mail and route packages.

World War II brought soldiers to Frisco, the hardy, hand-picked skiing soldiers of Colorado's famous Tenth Mountain Division, who trained at Camp Hale below nearby Tennessee Pass. The mountain

Frisco's 1940s postmaster Bob Foote (left) cuts beaver pond ice with friend for summer use.

109

troops later fought the Germans in the Italian Alps, seizing Mt. Belvedere on a dark, frozen night in 1945. They trained in the Ten Mile Canyon, living on C rations in the mountains from Fremont Pass north to Willow Creek, near today's Silverthorne. Friscoans say that 700 men camped in the North Ten Mile Canyon. Soldiers slipped into Frisco to buy candy at Chamberlain's Frisco Cafe, but found only dried fruit with a thin coating of cheap chocolate available. In November, 1943, the snack shop had been destroyed, victim of a disastrous fire started by an employee's kerosene spill. But a new cafe, complete with running water, opened next door in 1944.

When church and school bells all over America pealed the joyous news that the War had ended, sleepy Frisco stirred to new life. New people come to town and new things began to happen.

Robert S. and Helen Foote appeared in town in 1946 and bought the historic postoffice-store from Elmer Swanson. Foote labored to remodel the building, adding new tongue and groove walls, floors, woodwork. The cabin's exterior received a facelift,

A renovated 510 Main, with grocery and postoffice restored, opened in April, 1946 as Foote's Rest, a lodging for fishermen, hunters and summer vacationers. Robert S. Foote, who received an official postmaster's appointment on April 22, 1947, served postal patrons from the same window and brass boxes that Louis A. Wildhack had used.

At that time, the postoffice again emerged as a social center. Folks hungry for news arrived early, waited while the mail was put up and exchanged weather predictions, gossip, sickness and death notices, fire reports and political discussion. Bob Foote often personally delivered packages. If someone was sick, he would be sure to deliver their mail.

Bob and Helen Foote juggled washing sheets and cleaning cabins for guests with sorting mail, pumping gas and selling groceries. At Christmastime, they retreated to the comfort of their adjoining living room to sort the heavier mail load. Bob's mother, Hannah Mae Foote, nicknamed "Nonnie," helped with these chores and the Foote's family of four children. She became a cherished member of Frisco's town family. "I loved her and I think everyone did," recalled longtime resident Kenneth Caldwell.

A parade of local characters marched through the postoffice chatting with Nonnie and the Footes. Irish-born Chris Cluskey, Mary Ruth's father and a 1940s Frisco mayor, regaled the family with his "wild tales." Cluskey, who told stories of 1900s Breckenridge, impressed Helen Foote as "cute, a little short fella—and could he cuss!"

Reverend Harold Thompson

A man who found his strength in prayer, Reverend Harold Thompson lived on trust in God. He had little else. Once, Thompson and his wife Ethel knelt on their clean, flowered linoleum living room floor to pray for immediate cash to fix the preacher's Model A. In a matter of hours he needed to be 19 miles up the Canyon on Fremont Pass leading Sunday worship for workers at the Climax molybdenum mine, according to a June 11, 1950 *Denver Post* article. The pastor's total cash assets that day amounted to two cents—not enough to buy a repair job at the Frisco garage.

Soon, the Thompsons heard a knock. Their milkman, Harold Rutherford, stood sheepishly outside. "I got the feeling this morning I should come over here and pay my tithe. Here's three months," he said and pressed 85 cents into the pastor's hand. When Thompson later hurried his slight frame over to the Frisco shop to pick up the Ford, the bill came to 85 cents, plus 2 cents tax.

The Reverend made it on time to Climax.

"Be ye free from the love of money" (Hebrews 8:5), the Reverend's motto, made him refuse to pass the collection plate on Sundays. The "dear hearts and gentle people" of Frisco gave the Thompson family food and clothing. The intrepid Reverend often disappeared into the pine forest at Buffalo Mountain's base to hunt meat for the family stew pot. Despite his meager budget, Thompson managed to build a Christian boys camp, using lumber from an old hotel on Monarch Pass to construct a dormitory for 40 underprivileged boys. The fresh-faced exuberant campers flooded Frisco each summer and left full of the Thompson's homemade biscuits, bible stories and mosquito bites.

> They learned how to cooperate with each other, make their own beds, and keep their things in order. We hiked to the top of Mt. Royal, cooked out in the open, got acquainted with the outdoors. And I loaded them all into our 'new' old Dodge truck and took them on overnight camps up Vail pass.
>
> *The Denver Post*, June 11, 1950

"God never created a bad boy," the tireless Thompson confided. "They're full of spirit and that sometimes seems like wildness—until you steer it a little."

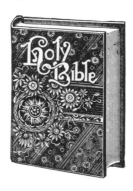

Susan Badger came into the postoffice and swapped stories in her crisp New England accent. Miss Badger, a "good story-teller with a command of the English language," loved books. Helen Foote handled the literate lady's constant flow of book club mailers. Despite her gentility, Miss Badger drove like a trucker. "She'd get back in her car, let the clutch out and rev that engine. She would roar around the corner" to her nearby home, Helen Foote said.

Along with the Foote family came the Porterfields, the Fails, the Marshes, Betty Cline and her son Virgil Landis. Ralph and Virginia Porterfield operated the Skyline Motel on the Smokin' Willy's site. Bill and Alma Fails built a cafe, the Blue Spruce restaurant, located on today's Chamber of Commerce site. They later leased the Frisco Cafe, built a cabin court and cafe called the A & B, built the Dairy King, now Butterhorn Bakery, and operated the Frisco Palms Cafe. Earl and Millie Marsh bought the Fail's A & B lodgings and operated it. Betty Cline and her son, Virgil Landis, refurbished the old Frisco Hotel and opened it to tourists.

Landis purchased the historic Frisco Hotel from longtime owner Lillian Wortman. The lodging belonged to the Linquists at the turn of the century. Landis, his mother and cousins, the Elams, along with local worker Clarence Burke, spent a year panelling the lobby in knotty pine, adding inside toilets, and remodeling rooms, plus building cabinets and tables to create a hotel worthy of its $3.50 per night rates on opening day, May 25, 1947. Landis remembered:

> It was right after the war and supplies were extremely hard to come by. One of the first things we had to learn was that mountain people were a very close knit group that didn't take to outsiders right off the bat so we had a hard time even getting things from Smith's Lumber Company and Western hardware in Leadville until we had done business with them for awhile. After that they couldn't do enough for us. Our first winter there was really an eyeopener for us as a winter in the Colorado Rockies cannot be described. It has to be experienced and lived. Since we were more or less in the process of tearing down and doing over we sort of roughed it you might say. The plumbing was of the outdoor variety. We boiled water in a big copper clothes boiler on the huge kitchen range and pulled our water from a well by means of a windlass. We were not exceptions as practically everyone else in town then did the same thing.

Landis highlighted an aspect of Frisco community life mentioned earlier by novelist Helen Rich: "Honestly, it does take about 20 years to be accepted in these mountain places." But Landis experienced Frisco's warmth long before that. Summing up his Frisco years, he said, "I wouldn't take a million dollars for the experience. I also wouldn't do it again for another million."

The town treasury reacted to all this activity by ballooning from a paltry $23.57 in 1944 to an impressive $1,022 in 1945. Suddenly, Frisco's town clerk experienced a flurry of lot sales. Town trustees felt so prosperous that they reinstated the clerk's salary: $2 per month.

Frisco's population swelled from a handful in 1940 to 50 in 1946, according to Virgil Landis. The town had one-seventh of Summit County's paltry 350 population. Almost every Friscoan turned out for Frank Ruth and Charley Lowe's town hall dances in the 1940s. These energetic party goers "raised so much dust" that dancers with respiratory problems had to stay home. Frisco's taste had turned from the pre-war "quadrille" (square dance) to elegant ballroom

Frisco Lodge owner Virgil Landis loved post-War Frisco's great outdoors. But winter's challenge in 350-strong mountain town proved grueling.

dancing. Oldtimers and newcomers both stopped one evening to watch Lula and Dimp Myers glide across the floor in a graceful Anniversary Waltz. "They danced beautifully," Helen Foote remembered.

Dimp Myers, a born clown who could be dignified or comical, once told friends about a midnight dance supper of oyster stew. "I put on my rubber boots and waded through the stuff—never did find an oyster."

Another high liver always carried a kerosene lamp to Frisco parties to guide him along the pitch-black path to his ranch home. This jovial soul, who sometimes over-indulged in spiritous drink, got so "likkered up" that when the dance ended after dawn, he lit up his kerosene lantern and stumbled home into the sunrise.

Frisco danced at beautiful Uneva Lake, too. Boats crossed the moonlit lake to a dance pavilion that later burned. Charles Lemming Tutt and Charles Morrison Pike Taylor had purchased Uneva around 1918 and Tutt bought Taylor's share from Alice Bemis Taylor after Taylor's death around 1920. The Tutts hired Frisco's Bill and Mary Ruth as caretakers in 1943.

The Ruths, despite their Uneva location, were included in Frisco's tight knit community. Nobody, not even a hotel owner like Virgil Landis, ever locked a door. "Frisco people used to be one big family," Cap Thompson said. "Everyone knew what everyone else's business was. If they didn't know today, they'd know tomorrow." "If we had a town or school election, we knew how each vote would come in," Helen Foote chuckled. "If anything changed the outcome, we knew who was responsible."

Frisco in the 1940s lived the western tradition of neighbors helping neighbors. "Everybody took care of everybody else," said Helen Foote. "My husband plowed snow for all the widowed ladies and the church." "If someone needed you during the night," said Susie Thompson, "you got up and went."

Frisco's own Florence Nightingale, Anne Woods, also responded during the night. Since the town had no doctor, Nurse Woods cared for the sick. "You called Anne or went and got Anne," Helen Foote recalled. "She came in her white cotton uniform, white nylon stockings and white nurse's shoes. She always wore a black cape. You felt better when she came in the door."

Those who ventured into town streets after dark no longer hazarded unseen potholes and bumps. Frisco boasted seven street lights in 1948.

The Ten Mile Canyon's well-known Wilfley Mine made *Denver*

115

Gas pump outside grocery-postoffice at 510 Main (left) anchored 1940s Frisco, a summer haven.

Post headlines December 1, 1938 with a big zinc strike. Area mining had blossomed in the late '30s with Henry Recen's new strike at the St. Louis near Kokomo and another at the Delaware Placers on Jacque Peak. Cap Thompson first found work in 1940 at a mine near Copper Mountain. The Wilfley continued to provide work for Frisco men in the late '40s. Virgil Landis remembered:

> I worked with Ben Staley at the old Wilfley Mine at Kokomo. We would get up to the mine a couple of hours before the shift came on and pump out the sumps so that when the miners came on duty, they would bar down and muck out. I ran a muck train and old Ben would do maintenance work... After the Wilfley played out, I got a job at Climax... running a muck train... six train loads a day. Going rate was... $1.54 an hour. Can say in retrospect that my job at Climax was the most exciting... in my fifty some years in the labor market.

Landis remembered stockpiling wood for the Frisco Hotel's winter use. He described buying a truckload of wood from nearby sawmills, such as the Frisco mill built by postmaster Elmer and son, Edward

Swanson. The cost? "Twenty- five cents a pickup load if you just backed up to the chute or fifty cents if you ricked it in yourself."

Frisco in the '40s had to prepare for winter's icy blast. Landis recalled, "The coldest I ever saw in Frisco was fifty-four degrees below zero. Even the fuel oil in the outside tanks would not run out." Frisco wound up the decade with the walloping 1949-50 winter, when residents shoveled snow up to second story windows. While parents cursed the overabundant white stuff, children hurrahed. For Frisco was back on skis and its youngsters rejoiced to lead the way.

Fast food (above) and fast drivers were both found in a changing Frisco.

117

CHAPTER 9

Growing Pains

Pull down the curtain, sit beside the lamp
Until the world within your eyeballs' arc
Rocks to its poise against the rushing dark.
(Belle Turnbull, *The Tenmile Range*)

When Norwegian Peter Prestrud arrived in Frisco in 1910 with his "yumping" skis, his zest for skiing spread like brushfire. Decades later, a coterie of avid skiers from Climax came to Frisco and ignited ski enthusiasm again—this time for downhill skiing.

The Jack Gorsuches (well known in Vail) and Jackie and Bill Pyles, along with Marie and Bob Zdechlik, the Bert Snyders, the Dick Wellingtons and others had pioneered local skiing at Climax's Chalk Mountain where lifts as early as 1938 put miners and their families on skis. Arapahoe Basin opened in 1946 and Breckenridge built a rope tow on its town park ski hill, still in use today. Somebody needed to light a fire under Frisco's 30-strong winter population.

Early efforts at putting Frisco's kids on skis came from enthusiastic parents. The Climax skiers, who moved to Frisco when the mine discontinued housing, provided the needed zest. "Jackie Pyles Evanger taught our kids to ski on Piston Hill and near the library and then took them to Breckenridge to ride the rope tow," Helen Foote related. Gil Gilkeson shuttled Frisco kids to the lifts in the 1950s:

> On weekends while the county was still small... we would go into Frisco, pile skis in the back of the pick-up and then pile kids on top of that and take off for Breckenridge... I guess half the town of Frisco learned to ski on that hill before we graduated to the big hills. We used to drive to the top of Vail Pass and ski down with someone picking us up at the bottom and driving us back up the hill.
>
> Gil Gilkeson, 1984 letter to Frisco Historical Society

Later, in the early 1960s, the school launched a ski instruction program that has opened an exciting new door for thousands of

Summit children. High school physical education instructor Larry Williams lamented the newly built high school's lack of a gym. School officials faced an accreditation roadblock without an athletic program. So Williams took his physical education classes to Summit's wintry white playground, and started a Summit schools ski instruction program. High school teacher Bert Snyder helped bus young skiers to Climax's Chalk Mountain, and Arapahoe Basin also welcomed the kids. The program that Willliams began got youngsters up on skis and continued in some cases through downhill race training or nordic competion. Years later Pat Ahern, 1984 winter Olympics contender, trained under present Summit school coach Gary Giberson on the Mt. Royal jump constructed by local residents.

Steve Rieschl, formerly Vail's nationally known cross-country ski proponent, appeared in a 1965 *Denver Post* photo leading a troupe of 17 Summit children on an early morning nordic tour to school in Frisco. Rieschl, then school director of physical education, boasted 140 children in his ski program. He, and successors Jim Balfanz, Jim Mattson and Gary Giberson, introduced local kids to ski jumping, first on a hill at Farmers Korner, then at a jump site on the Maryland Creek Ranch. Reischl also began local competitive meets.

Rudd and Scott Pyles made the U.S. ski team in the 1960s.
Courtesy Marie Zdechlik

"We used to take (our son, Zane) into school at 6:00 in the morning and the kids would all meet with the ski coach and cross country before school. He also competed in ski jumping," Gil Gilkeson said.

Jody Anderson, Frisco Lodge owner, and Marie Zdechlik organized a group of 14 mothers to teach 120 local kids beginner ski skills. Before the grade schoolers tackled Arapahoe, the mothers prepared them on the hill near the high school bus barns, where Jody and Marie had cleared the trees. Some volunteer instructors graduated to the Arapahoe ski program site with their small pupils. "We used to buy an Arapahoe Basin ski pass for the lodge, which I used, and school children skied for 50 cents at Arapahoe," said Jody Anderson.

These happy years of practice paid off. Beryl Palmer was the first of many to compete in the Junior Nationals, in 1967. David Bristol and Beryl Palmer qualified for the biathalon in the Army. Rudd and Scott Pyles raced in slalom and downhill events. A number of Frisco kids made the U. S. Ski Team. Frisco sent a skier to the Olympics, Twila Hinkle in 1976.

Frisco's interest in Nordic skiing led to the creation of Colorado's first citizens' race in the late 1960s. The Frisco Gold Rush, launched by Jody Anderson, is today the state's oldest cross country citizens' event and one of its most popular.

Frisco rarely lacked snow for its alpine activities. Author Helen Rich, in an *Empire* magazine article, recorded 18 feet of the white stuff between October, 1950 and July, 1951. The July storm would be what Miss Rich called a "willow bender." In 1952, the *Summit County Journal* reported 12 feet of snowfall by February 8, impressive for mid-winter. Summit's heaviest snowfalls usually come late, in March and April.

Frisco Feudin' Fifties

Seeds of bitterness sowed themselves in Frisco's peaceful environs in the 1950s. Dillon Reservoir spawned dissension in Frisco. After the new lake submerged area ranches, road builders commandeered a pathway through the new ranch locations. Tempers also flared over re-locating the school to Dillon in 1952. But the first bitter episode began over a barbed wire fence that severed Frisco's graveyard.

The squabble began when newcomer Emil Slovak bought an east Frisco ranch bordering the burial ground. Slovak, hired as Frisco's new schoolteacher, studied his deed and determined that he owned one half-acre within cemetery grounds. Armed with this conviction and a total lack of diplomacy, the territorial-minded schoolteacher erected an offensive fence and nailed No Trespassing signs on every post. Nellie Thomas Mogee, whose pioneer mother, a brother and infant son resided in the cemetery, burst into tears at the news. Enraged Frisco citizens tore down Slovak's fence, which had disturbed Conrad Ecklund's grave, and ripped off his odious signs.

Then they marched into Judge William Luby's district court demanding a restraining order against Slovak—and got it.

Nellie's 70-year old husband, rancher Dan Mogee, led the fight against the disruptive Mr. Slovak. "There have been dozens of owners on the ranch since 1880 and they all knew about this, and would not try to take it from us," Mogee declared in an October 14, 1951 *Rocky Mountain News* interview. Fifty-five year Summit resident Wib Giberson backed him up. "We're going to see this thing through the courts," he said. "This is the first time in 70 years someone has made a complaint against us."

Twenty-seven year old Emil Slovak, who soon vacated his Frisco teaching position to teach in Montezuma, viewed the problem this way:

> I hadn't planned to do anything about [the cemetery] until these people irritated me. My wife offered [the cemetery land] for $2400 and the board just laughed at her and told her they could condemn the property. That's when I hired a lawyer. Strangers are not accepted easily here.

Slovak lost his case, dismantled the remains of his barbed-wire fence, under duress, and slunk off into the sunset, after selling the ranch to Merle Stewart. Stewart left the graveyard alone.

School Squabble

Frisco's 50-year old log schoolhouse said goodbye to its apple pie Americana innocence in the 1950s. Things were still sweet in 1951 when Emma Sawyer taught 16 children in the single-room school. But when January, 1952 ushered in a New Year, dissension arose. A group of 32 citizens signed a petition to dissolve Frisco's 70-year old school district and send Frisco's 16 students to the larger, more modern Dillon school. County schools superintendent Lilias P. Stafford responded, according to Colorado law, by calling a special election for February 21, 1952 to determine the school district's fate. Feelings ran high in Frisco. Parents who defended the integrity of the local school and refused to let Frisco become a ghost town butted horns with those who desired the safety of a school bus and the

121

convenience of a warm school with indoor toilets. Neighbors who had known each other for years refused to speak on the street. Finally a 33 to 26 vote against dissolving the district saved the Frisco school. Jubilant kids rang the big school bell to announce election results for a *Denver Post* photo.

High Altitude High Jinks

Their feuding finished, townsfolk turned their attention to a new threat. A foray against an intruder occurred when a strange character rattled the doors of Frisco matrons at night, causing widespread fear among the women of the town. Gil Gilkeson, appointed Summit County Sheriff to complete the term of Sheriff Ray Loomis who had died, set out to capture this menace. As the ladies of Frisco shivered with fright, Gilkeson and his men staked out the town. Night came and darkness thickened. Suddenly Gilkeson and his deputy caught sight of a burly black figure approaching the door of a Galena Street home. Just as the deputy readied himself to pounce on the powerful figure, he turned—and Gilkeson recognized the intruder as a big

Beloved Frisco teacher Vodie Fletcher poses with 1950s pupils outside a schoolhouse soon to yield to "progress".

122

black bear. The animal was rubbing against the doorknob to scratch himself. The U. S. Forest Service transferred the midnight rattler to another location and once more Frisco's women slept.

Stories of bears and mountain lions who raided Frisco's garbage cans failed to daunt Frisco's finest fishermen who toted fishing poles and bait to the "Kids' Pond" near the ski jump. Fishing: Age 14 and Under said the sign posted at the kids' pond. The kids' catch usually provided dinner, because the Fish and Game warden regularly stocked the pond with trout.

Another "catch" for local children came out of the North Ten Mile, where shepherds pastured flocks in summer. After the fall round-up, the Bristol boys captured the left-overs and brought them home. Once they chased a stray ewe and lamb toward the Curtin ponds. The ewe broke through thin ice into a beaver pond and her wool got so wet and heavy that the boys couldn't pull her out. Luckily, the Enyeart brothers stopped their car on the highway and came to the young rustler's rescue.

Snaring trout and abandoned sheep were o.k. for the Bristol boys, but their first Frisco winter an uninvited family of skunks took up residence beneath the family's kitchen floor to the childrens' dismay. A skunk fight erupted. When young Bonnie Bristol entered the schoolroom next day, someone said "I smell skunk!" The embarrassed Bonnie flushed and kept her mouth shut tight.

Summertime lent itself to escapades, but winter brought adventure of a different kind. When mountain roadways turned treacherous during blizzards, Frisco lent its town hall to house stranded motorists. Edna Wells Jones remembers a Labor Day, 1961 storm when people opened homes and businesses to snowbound travelers. Charles Chamberlain never slept those nights, keeping his Frisco gas station open so that travelers could warm up and buy gas or tire chains. "Sometimes people would bang on our door in the middle of the night because they needed gas," Mickie Chamberlain Carabello wrote. "Dad would get up and get them what they needed."

Winter ushered in a ritual for the Foote family. They cut huge blocks of ice from Frisco's frozen beaver ponds each February and stored it surrounded by sawdust in an ice house to sell to summer visitors. Ice cutting is an old-fashioned activity. Summit's early residents used to cut ice for summer use and splurge their supply on July 4 ice cream making. The Foote's huge ice saw, long missing, has recently returned to Frisco for museum display.

Some people still toted pails of water from the town spring in the

1950s, when the rest of America relaxed before TV sets and ran hot tub baths. The Bristols laughed about a nighttime trip to the unlit spring. A family member returned from the spring, plunked a full bucket down on the kitchen floor—and noticed a fish flapping in the water!

At Last! Frisco Finances Water Plant

Running water finally flowed into Frisco town water mains in 1955 when the town gritted its economic teeth and issued a $40,000 bond, the absolute limit for a town with Frisco's less-than-100 population. Most everyone had wells and installed electric pumps for indoor running water, but sometimes in winter hand-dug wells went dry due to a low water table. Perforated pipes were laid in the North Ten Mile Creek. Water ran crystal clear and pure. Frisco rejoiced in its reliable water supply.

Dillon Reservoir

The Denver Water Board had for decades dreamed of harnessing Summit's three rushing rivers for the city's burgeoning water growth needs. During Depression years, beginning in 1929, the water board quietly bought land from financially-strapped Dillon residents, people unable to raise tax payments. By the 1940s, The Denver Water Board owned most of Dillon and gained power to condemn land for its reservoir. In 1956, the board dropped a bombshell that shocked not only Dillonites but also Frisco ranch families like the Gibersons. Homes and businesses must vacate by 1961. Soon survey crews crowded the area. Workers bored the 23-mile long Harold D. Roberts diversion tunnel through the Continental Divide to carry water from the three rivers confluence to the Eastern Slope. Men and machines moved into mow down the pine forests surrounding Dillon and Frisco.

Soon water flooded the eastern meadows of Frisco's big mountain park location and water lapped at the town boundaries. Roadways were rerouted and buildings, such as Dillon's Antlers Cafe and Holiday House (later Peak One Motel) were moved.

Dillon dam and reservoir construction flooded the area with worker families, a strain on sleepy Summit's capacity to provide housing and services. Frisco began to look like a trailer town. Population swelled with construction, then sagged after the dam was topped off, July 18, 1963. Water recreation tourism and lakeside condominiums that sprang up after Lake Dillon filled in 1965 inflated the balloon again. While the reservoir's general effect was to boost

Mary Ruth

1902-

When Mary Ruth's father, Christopher P. Cluskey came to Breckenridge around 1900 from Trim, County Meath, Ireland, he had a mischievous twinkle in his eye. His boyhood sweetheart, Mary Elizabeth Coughlin, arrived soon to marry Chris in Breckenridge and attempt to settle him down. Everyone in Summit County knew colorful Chris and Lizzie.

Mary, their oldest child, arrived in 1902. She began school in Breckenridge's old Masonic Hall, attended in Dillon around 1912 and finished at the Slate Creek School. Mary Ruth remembered, "Every Saturday night there was a dance in Frisco or Dillon. Name any kind of dance and we did it."

Cooking for miners at the famous Pennsylvania Mine in Peru Creek, the old company mine town of Tiger near Breckenridge, the Jessie in Gold Run Gulch and atop Boreas Pass kept Mary Ellen Cluskey busy after school days ended. During the tragic 1918 influenza epidemic, when her father hauled bodies to the mortuary, Mary had the flu three times, but managed to survive.

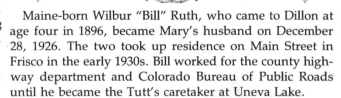

Maine-born Wilbur "Bill" Ruth, who came to Dillon at age four in 1896, became Mary's husband on December 28, 1926. The two took up residence on Main Street in Frisco in the early 1930s. Bill worked for the county highway department and Colorado Bureau of Public Roads until he became the Tutt's caretaker at Uneva Lake.

Mary buried her brother, Chris, during the War, in December, 1944 and in 1945 her invalid mother and a niece, Theresa, died. On July 6, 1945, sorrow turned to joy. Mary welcomed home her son, Bernard, a U. S. Army soldier, just released from a Nazi prison camp.

Chris Cluskey served "at least two terms as Frisco's mayor," according to his December 4, 1953 *Summit County Journal* obituary. Bill Ruth died the next year. Mary Ruth launched her town career in 1955 with 15 years as Frisco town clerk.

Mary lived in Frisco until recent years when she retired to her son, Bernard's, home in Texas. She liked to remember her childhood in a young Summit County.

"We picked gooseberries after the Fourth of July, then strawberries, raspberries and black currants at Argentine Pass." Mary remembered riding the railroad home from school in Dillon, Prestrud driving the Kremmling stagecoach and seeing the famous 13-pound gold nugget, "Tom's Baby," at Smith's Jewelry in Breckenridge. "I only saw it once," she said. "It was on the Fourth of July and we had the worst snowstorm you can imagine!"

Frisco's economy—and to provide jobs for locals like excavator Wayne Bristol—its construction caused confusion and strife. One result: Population shifts and political manipulation closed Frisco's old school.

Frisco's growing student population seemed secure in the early '50s. The school had divided into two rooms by 1954. Virginia Alexander, who lived in an attic apartment above the schoolhouse with her family, presided over upper grades, fourth through eighth. Euvodia Fletcher taught the younger children. "Vodie" Fletcher became the source of many happy memories, like this one from Gil Gilkeson about his son's school days:

> Our son Jay went to school (in the old school house) to Vodie Fletcher. She was hardly taller than her students. On Halloween she would have her children make brown paper bag masks and then she would lead them down the street in single file (she resembled the Pied Piper) and they would go trick or treating to all the widow ladies and older people early in the afternoon who would have goodies baked and waiting for them to come.

Storm clouds began to brew. Dam workers, clustered around Dillon and the new town of Silverthorne, caused Summit's population base to shift northward. Suddenly, Summit's only high school, in Breckenridge, seemed misplaced. People began to demand centrally located schools.

Frisco's Helen Foote, hired in 1958 to set up a new home economics department at the Summit High School in Breckenridge, kept an exhaustive news clipping file on the school location fracas. Events unfolded this way in 1962:

- Dillon's 170-pupil elementary school awaits the wrecker's ball as Denver Water Board officials prepare to flood the old Dillon site.

- Breckenridge's elementary school, a converted residence, is pronounced "educationally unsound" by Summit school officials.

- The Colorado Industrial Commission condemns Breckenridge's 1909-built brick high school as structurally unsafe. A Denver structural engineer declares that the building could collapse with high wind, falling ice or earth tremor conditions.

- Summit County voters turn down a $395,000 school bond issue to fund new county schools construction by a 206 to

126 vote.

- When the school board taps capital reserve funds to begin construction on an elementary school building on U. S. Forest Service land near Frisco, taxpayers slap the board with a lawsuit and obtain an August 9, 1962 court injunction to halt work on the new structure.

A distraught Summit County School Superintendent Robley E. Aspegren complained to a Denver Post reporter, "The people are going to have to get on the ball and decide they need schools or I'm going to be the only superintendent in Colorado without any schools."

Mothers March

As the September, 1962 school term approached, an impassioned group of placard-waving Summit County mothers, tots in arms or tripping behind, marched to Colorado Governor Steve McNichols' State Capitol office. Earning newspaper headlines and photos, they pleaded with the governor to take a hand in their school dispute. Some mothers returned in tears because McNichols protested that his hands were tied. An August 25, 1962 *Rocky Mountain News* editorial, the day following the march, backed the governor, saying, "...this is essentially a local problem... that the courts can untangle."

Meanwhile Summit County kids from Frisco, Dillon and Breckenridge started school in an ill-suited assortment of Frisco buildings probably worse than those razed and condemned. Parents hurried to scrub down and paint Frisco's old Town Hall. Reverend Thompson's abandoned Rocky Mountain Bible Church boys camp dorm was pressed into service. Frisco's metal Armco building housed students and more crammed into the old log schoolhouse. Students also crowded into a two-room building transported from Breckenridge.

Helen Foote had no running water for home economics cooking classes. Bert Snyder's voice carried through thin walls to nearby classrooms. Children caught cold walking between buildings in deep snow. Parents worried about leg growth malformations because children's feet became so cold that they sat with feet tucked beneath on their chairs all day.

Finally, the fracas ended, with Summit County citizens' agreement to proceed with the present lakeside school complex at Frisco. Two classroom rotundas at Frisco opened; one in 1963 accommodated elementary students. In 1964, high schoolers moved into their rotunda facility, lacking cafeteria and gymnasium facilities. Indoor gym classes took place in rotunda common areas and soccer practice on the rocky cow pasture where the Safeway store now stands. The school ski team, however, had a perfect practice field: Arapahoe Basin.

Between 1966 and 1970, bond issues funded a gym, music rooms, cafeteria, science rooms and school library, plus an elementary school. County enrollment rose to 550 by decade's end.

Was condemnation of the Breckenridge High School a political ploy? When Colorado Mountain College renovated the 1909 building in the late seventies, College director Sue Daley called in structural engineers to check the building's solidarity. "Built solid as a bunker," they declared. "You could fill that gym floor with dancing elephants and it wouldn't collapse."

Leaving its troubled times behind, Frisco stepped into a new era of growth and change. Kansas' Rounds & Porter Company had opened a ski area on Breckenridge's Peak 8 and rumors of a ski resort at Copper Mountain had surfaced. Vail's debut in 1962 brought a trickle of skier traffic to Frisco, as the town's early day crossroads role began to revive. The historic Frisco Lodge, purchased by the Charles Andersons from J. D. and Mary McLucas in June, 1961, became a barometer of Frisco's tourism. Its 1940s owner, Virgil Landis, had declared that after Labor Day "a curtain dropped" over Summit County and visitors simply stopped coming. In the '60s, according to Jody Anderson, winters brightened somewhat with skier business, but lodge owners still struggled to stay alive. "Summers were very busy," said Jody, "except for the year of Colorado's devastating Platte River flood, 1965. *No one* came that summer."

Frisco approached the end of the sixties formulating plans for a sanitation district that would install the town's first sewer system. Nine-year town mayor Charles Anderson shepherded the project to completion in 1969.

The town applauded its proud new postoffice in October, 1966. Postmaster Susan L. Thompson supervised the move from the antique station at Foote's Rest, remembering its year-round rental of 12-15 post boxes when she first arrived in 1938.

The Frisco Volunteer Fire Department reorganized in 1966, according to a '60s news tabloid, The *Frisco Peaker*. Fire Chief Jim Smith washed his hands of the old system, born of bucket brigade days, when Frisco's menfolk ran helter-skelter to quench a blaze. Regular volunteer meetings, training sessions and assigned responsibility for fire equipment maintenance upgraded town fire protection.

FRISCO!

Talk of Interstate 70 bisecting Frisco's ranchlands and by-passing the town, tearing up the narrow Ten Mile Canyon, buzzed among townspeople, but Frisco remained undisturbed. The beautiful canyon still provided "fishing, picnicking and digging around for ruins," a favorite Gilkeson family activity.

Other former Friscoans shared that enthusiasm for Frisco's Canyon playground. Mickie Chamberlain Carabello described teenage fun in the '60s:

> My favorite memory is going to the Well House. Every kid in Frisco went there. It seemed so private. From there we would go to the river. The kids in Frisco used to say they were going to the sand dunes... We would innertube down the river in our cut-offs and bathing suits. The water was just as cold then as it is now, but we thought it wasn't bad. There was an old cable that crossed the river, up behind Mt. Royal. It had a cart... on it. We would spend hours on it.

In a few years distant, Interstate Highway 70 construction teams would change the course of the Ten Mile to squeeze the divided highway into the tight canyon. Cable car and sand dunes would disappear then. But Frisco in the 1960s, for the time being, retained its links to the past.

Frisco native Carl Prestrud joined Colorado governor Richard Lamm in celebrating Frisco's Main Street renovation.

CHAPTER 10

Looking Back To Look Forward

The logs have been sealed away and overlaid
Paper on paper. You long to peel the stuff,
The flowered, the plain, the dearbought dim brocade,
Down to the muslin, down to the old buff,
Down to whatever is left of a man dead,
A bit of wool maybe dyed with butternut
Caught in a mitered corner, a hair of him shed,
Or sweet in the wood the name of a girl cut.
There's not a man of a ledger to tell his name
Or whether he hewed from lodgepole or spruce or fir,
But wherever his bones are on the range or the plain
Here in old years his bones and his brains were.
Every time a nail strikes into the chinking,
Into the hollow of time, it will set you thinking.
(Belle Turnbull, *The Tenmile Range*)

Frisco took a great leap forward in the years from 1970 to present. The '70s focused on "Get ready," and "Get set." When 1980 came, citizens said "Go!" Frisco sprang forth in an explosive thrust of growth and activity that overnight transformed the town to an energetic Summit County leader. When Friscoans updated Frisco, they did it with an eye on the past, in the tradition of a "big family" community.

Everything pointed to growth for Frisco. The new Copper Mountain ski area opened in November, 1972. The Summit County library built its main branch in Frisco. Interstate 70 progressed from the Silverthorne interchange to Frisco in the early '70s, then penetrated the Ten Mile Canyon to mount Vail Pass. New restaurants, businesses and lodgings sprang up near I-70 exit 203. The Summit Medical Center opened. The Best Western joined the Holiday Inn, Safeway and the Summit County Bank built along old Colorado Highway 9/North Main Street, today renamed Summit Blvd. Frisco worked to form a fire protection district in 1973, culminating in the new Frisco Fire Station, completed in 1981, housing an array of modern firefighting vehicles and equipment. A new Frisco Elementary School was underway at Bill's Ranch and Frisco's Summit High School added a second gym and vocational wing in 1973, then its beautiful auditorium and swimming pool in 1975. Longtime teachers who remembered the cramped quarters of earliers days—among them Virginia Alexander, Phyllis Armstrong, Elizabeth Culbreath, Helen Foote, Clarence and Phyllis (New) LaBarr, Harry Skaro, Hubert Snyder and Bernadine Wellington—sighed in relief at the school's completion.

"The 1970s were a time of laying down infrastructure for future growth," Frisco Mayor Douglas P. Jones explained in an April, 1984 interview. While nearby Summit towns such as Breckenridge and Silverthorne struggled to cope with runaway 1970s growth—in construction, services, town government, utilities, roads—Frisco paused. "No new building went up on Main Street from around 1972 to 1982," said Doug Jones. "Frisco was watching its sister towns and learning. When growth did come, we didn't have to try to catch up."

The town paved its streets in 1974, to the delight of homeowners. Frisco consolidated its water resources by increasing its already excellent water rights to prepare for future growth and expanding its water production facilities. Today, four wells, a 1,370,000 gallon storage capacity and a 1980 water treatment plant handle one million gallons of North Ten Mile Creek water per day, with a two million capacity. (The water plant is dedicated to Wayne E. Bristol.) The Sanitation District plant can treat one million gallons every day. In 1978, the town board asked the electorate to approve a two percent sales tax hike. The money from this approved tax boost financed the large scale improvements of the 1980s.

"Ready, Set, *Grow!*"

A maverick mentality in 1980 set the pace for innovations in Frisco's approach to development. That mentality led to grassrooots citizen participation in Frisco's renovation. The free-thinking town fathers first demonstrated their independent spirit by rejecting federal revenue sharing funds in 1980. The move made national headlines. Town trustees discovered under the glare of public attention that the U.S. government had no provision for an upstart little town like Frisco to turn down its grant. The town had to accept the money, but set a policy of refusing to rely on outside funds that may dry up—as revenue sharing funds are today.

Captain S. and
Susan L. Thompson

S panning an era that starts with a sleepy mountain hamlet in the late '30s and reaches to the dynamic Summit County crossroads community of today, Cap and Susie Thompson's time in Frisco has been a period of change.

The Thompsons arrived in Frisco from Nebraska in 1938. Cap went to work at a mine on the Ten Mile Canyon's Medicine Creek, south of Copper Mountain in 1940. They lived with their two-year old son, Loren, in an old mine cabin. The Thompsons found Frisco a town imprisoned in its 1900s past— no indoor plumbing, no electricity, no running water and limited telephone service in an isolated, often snowbound, mountain hideaway. Summer residents through 1941, the Thompsons purchased their Fourth Avenue home in 1945. They helped rebuild Frisco's gathering place, the Frisco Cafe, after a disastrous 1943 fire wiped out owners Ken and Betty Chamberlain. Cap joined Public Service Company in 1945 and the family moved to Dillon to live at the company's hydroelectric plant, located where today's ballfields are, below Dillon Dam.

Sue Thompson worked in the Dillon postoffice and later became Frisco postmaster in August, 1965, following Robert Foote's retirement. She managed the move from the antiquated Wildhack-era postal station to Frisco's new Granite Street postoffice in June, 1966.

A warm relationship grew between the Thompsons and their well-known neighbor, Susan Emery Badger. She shared her well water with the newcomers. Susie became a frequent guest for afternoon tea, a formal affair served with the finest of china cups. In later years, the Thompsons filled a divided plate with food, especially at holiday time, that the elderly lady enjoyed in her own home. Miss Badger often laughed about the dividends she received when she gave Susie the plate.

As Frisco approached its centennial, Susan Thompson led efforts to preserve the century-old silver town's history. She and Sue Chamberlain worked to assemble and display a Frisco historical exhibit in 1979. The collection, debuted at the Chamber of Commerce building, July 4, 1979 and again displayed in the Town Hall on Labor Day weekend, offered photographs, letters from old-timers, maps and artifacts for public view. These donations grew into the Frisco Historical Park museum's present collection.

A newly-formed Frisco Historic Commission launched a project aimed to preserve and re-locate historic buildings, such as the Bailey House, the log schoolhouse and the Bill's Ranch house. On July 2, 1983, the Frisco Historic Park opened. The same day, the Frisco Historical Society became a legal body and elected Susan L. Thompson its first president.

Later that year, when Cap and Susie Thompson celebrated their 50th wedding anniversary, Frisco and Nebraska friends cooperated to create a hand-stitched quilt commemorating a half-century of commitment to family, friends, Frisco and to each other, a colorful tribute to the longtime Frisco couple. Their son Loren passed away July 23, 1980. His widow, Sharron, and two children, Julie and Brad, live in Frisco.

Already marching to the beat of a different drummer, Frisco set about shaking its century-old community out of stagnation. Newly-elected mayor Doug Jones and his town board in September, 1980 invited the people of Frisco to get into the act with a "Citizens of Frisco Planning Frisco" program. Three initial task force meetings drew 120 of Frisco's 1200 residents into an adventure in participatory government. Townspeople were asked to identify Frisco's problems—and they did—and to get involved, hands on, in their solution. The brainstorming sessions used playful approaches such as The Un-Secrets Map. This exercise asked, "What do you know about Frisco that no one else knows?" Six or seven people in each group teamed up to create information-packed maps. "We learned an incredible amount about the town," Jones said. Another device, The Good and Bad Map, charted Frisco's beauty spots and blemishes. The groups also indulged their wildest fantasies for Frisco's restoration with an Ideal Map; it freed citizens from money and other restraints to dream up town transformation. But The Realistic Map requested residents to work with budgets, known resources and exising town layout to realize their dreams.

"From these three meetings, we identified five major citizen concerns," said Jones. People's priorities were:

Babying aged log buildings became an art during transport of historic structures to Frisco's 1983-opened Frisco Historic Park.

- A facelift for Main Street
- A parks and recreation plan
- Preservation of Frisco's history
- A master plan to guide growth
- Revised zoning ordinances for innovative development

But citizen involvement didn't stop there. Five committees formed and rolled up their collective sleeves to attack the work before them. The Main Street committee, for example, tackled the challenge of transforming roadway ownership from the State Highway Department to the town, as well as shopping for the perfect street light—a modern "mine timber"-mounted globe won out. Citizens insisted on hooks for banners, flags and Christmas greenery on the lamp posts and specified electric outlets to plug in holiday lights.

"Their concerns were critical," Jones said. "There was no filtering of their requests through the bureaucracy. What they said was what they got."

A little girl at one of the task force sessions said she couldn't see around parked cars when she stepped out to cross Main Street. What she got was street corners that "bulge" out to provide pedestrians a clear look down the street.

Main Street committee members fussed over building heights and setbacks, sidewalk layout, pavers (they ended up with brick), plus an overall design image that said "Frisco"—not Breckenridge, Vail or Central City—and worked until they got it right. As plans progressed, businessmen and homeowners launched new construction, remodeling and addition projects, responding to a "ripple effect" that got people moving.

Meanwhile, Frisco's $1.2 million town hall, enhanced by a sunny indoor atrium and imposing bell tower, moved to completion on West Main Street. When Governor Richard Lamm stepped from his helicopter October 1, 1982 to help dedicate Frisco's new Main Street, the entire party of dignitaries and guests took a gala walk from the street's east boundary to the newly completed Frisco town hall.

Other committees achieved rousing results. A sound master plan and creative zoning ordinances received Town Board approval. The parks group witnessed the creation of a new bike path network linked to the Vail Pass-Ten Mile Canyon National Recreation Trail bikeway and saw the completion of Walter Byron Memorial Park, situated on a bike trail. (Frisco is a crossroads on two national cross-country bike routes.) The Historical Committee identified 59 historic buildings and sites in Frisco, then obtained and restored several to create the Frisco Historic Park in 1983. A new non-profit corporation, the Frisco Historical Society, formed to accept donations of historical documents, photographs and artifacts and to house the collection in the newly-acquired log schoolhouse museum. The schoolhouse in January, 1984 received listing on the National Register of Historic Places. The 1880s jail and four historic residences occupy the park. The committee chose a "living history" concept for the park, which today houses artisans including a leatherworker, silver and goldsmith, weaver, potter and fine artist. A general store with natural foods and a Colorado Mountain College office complete the list of those using the restored buildings in 1984. The Frisco Historical Society commissioned this historical book, also in 1984.

Looking Forward

Frisco, with its 1983 population of 1,509, stands today as a crossroads, a pivotal position the town held a hundred years ago in the 1880s. Though 70 percent of Frisco's residential units belong to second homeowners, most of these are Colorado front range residents, according to Doug Jones. "These people come every weekend and participate in town activities," he said. "They have a sense of identity with this town." Frisco's image, Jones asserts, is not that of a resort town, but a "homogeneous small town with lots of things going on."

Frisco's future holds the promise of an exciting new Nordic ski park that aims to become "the premiere cross-country center in the western United States," according to Doug Jones. He points out Frisco's historic love for the sport. The Nordic center, anchored just south of town near the ski jumps, will utilize a myriad of cross country ski trails in the area and add connecting links, developing a trail system in Frisco and its surrounding mountains. Three base areas will serve skiers at the Peninsula Campground, a meadow north of town and at the Nordic (jump) site. There, 49 acres, under land trade negotiations with the U. S. Forest Service, will house a service area with restaurant, accessory sales, ski rental, Nordic ski school and rest areas. Two ponds nearby will serve skaters, while the existing jumps will undergo technical improvements.

A citizens' group has brainstormed the center concept and will launch a design competition for its physical creation. Frisco will seek a business or non-profit organization from the private sector to assist in financing and operating the proposed Nordic center. Enthusiasm for the project runs high. "We're going to set the standards," said Jones.

Frisco, Summit's century-old silver town, experienced a roller-coaster cycle of economic ups and downs. The town soared in the 1880s, the 1900s, and sank to near nothing during Depression years. When Frisco reached its lowest point, the town drew together to create a community spirit that could not be quenched—not by hardship during its bleakest days nor by explosive growth in recent years. When its citizens came together to forge a new Frisco, they reaffirmed the community's deep roots in Western open-handedness, friendliness and interdependence, as well as a maverick nonconformity. Land use planners queried a citizens' task force group about their ideas for Frisco's image. They asked, "What do you want Frisco to look like?" The answer came back, "Itself!"

Frisco is primarily a place for its own people. Its attractiveness to second homeowners and visitors comes from its splendid Colorado mountain location and from its own special brand of integrity, for Frisco is "Itself!"

Sue Chamberlain, born on the family's Giberson ranch near Frisco donned antique finery to honor 100-year old Frisco.